CARRY ON IN FAITH

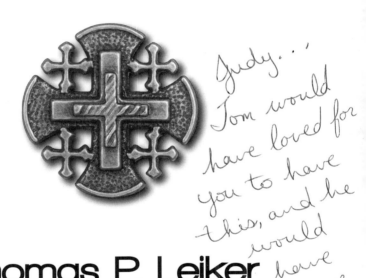

Thomas P. Leiker

Liguori, Missouri

Imprimi Potest:
Harry Grile, CSsR, Provincial
Denver Province, The Redemptorists

Published by Liguori Publications
Liguori, Missouri 63057

To order, call 800-325-9521
www.liguori.org

Copyright © 2013 Thomas P. Leiker

All rights reserved. No part of this publication may be reproduced, stored in a retrieval system, or transmitted in any form or by any means—electronic, mechanical, photocopy, recording, or any other—except for brief quotations in printed reviews, without the prior written permission of Liguori Publications.

Cataloging-in-Publication Data on file with the Library of Congress

p ISBN 9780764822155

e ISBN 9780764822940

Scripture texts in this work are taken from the *New American Bible*, revised edition © 2010, 1991, 1986, 1970 Confraternity of Christian Doctrine, Washington, D.C., and are used by permission of the copyright owner. All Rights Reserved. No part of the *New American Bible* may be reproduced in any form without permission in writing from the copyright owner.

Compliant with *The Roman Missal*, third edition.

Liguori Publications, a nonprofit corporation, is an apostolate of The Redemptorists. To learn more about The Redemptorists, visit Redemptorists.com.

Printed in the United States of America
17 16 15 14 13 / 5 4 3 2 1
First Edition

Days and Moments
A Table of Contents

Preface: Another Book About the Passion?	5
Reflecting Theologically	6

Part I: The Last Days With Jesus   9

An Intense Human Experience	9
To Touch the Hem of Jesus' Garment	10
Lazarus' House	12
Bartimaeus and Zacchaeus	13
Palm Sunday	16
Monday of Holy Week	18
Cleansing the Temple	19
Teaching Tuesday	22
Tuesday Night and the Eschatological Discourse	25
The Petition to Arrest Jesus	27
Judas and the Sanhedrin	29
Holy Thursday of the Lord's Supper	31
The First Eucharist	32
Jesus Serves His Followers	34
The Last Discourses	36
The Advocate	39
The Longest Day There Ever Was	41
Trials	43
Who Is Barabbas?	46
The Sentence	50
On the Cross	52
The Burial of Jesus	55

Part II: The First Days With Jesus — 59

Who Is Mary Magdalene? — 59
Easter Sunday: As Morning Breaks — 62
The Aftermath — 65
Emmaus: A Road to Life — 66
Our Hearts Were Burning — 68
Second Sunday of Easter — 71
The Real Saint Thomas — 73
Jesus Appears in Galilee — 75
Love One Another — 77
Ascending — 79
Come, O Holy Spirit — 81
And They Were Filled With the Holy Spirit — 84
Peter — 87
The Apostles Among the People — 89
James — 92
The Hard Lessons — 95

Part III: Every Day With Jesus — 99

The Remembrance — 99
The Bread of Life — 101

Preface
Another Book About the Passion?

Another book about the passion? Really? What makes this one any different than the others? Most of what Christians know or think they know about the passion and death of our Lord Jesus Christ comes from the four canon gospels. Sometimes the story is read while the faithful observe from a distance. The Catholic Church celebrates the reading of the passion on both Palm Sunday and Good Friday. On Palm Sunday, the synoptic gospels of Matthew, Mark, and Luke are interpreted in correspondence to their year in a three-year cycle of Scripture readings. On Good Friday every year, the story comes from the Gospel of John. The stories for Holy Thursday, Easter Sunday, and the Second Sunday of Easter also come from John. As Lent becomes Holy Week, which becomes Easter, the Church relies heavily on John to tell the story from the tremendous teaching experience at the Last Supper, through the torturous passion and death, on to the resurrection, and the return of the Lord.

For the Good Friday reading, the faithful are often called on to shout the words of a faceless crowd, most notably, "Crucify him! Crucify him!" In that way, the modern-day followers of Christ have a connection, even if minimal, with his followers in gospel time. *Carry on in Faith* steps beyond the confines of the Holy Gospels, still relying heavily on John and the other evangelists, but reaching into more of the history that was also part of the story that we now celebrate as Holy Week and the entire Easter season through Pentecost, the last and the first days. Who were these people—the apostles, Caiaphas, Pilate, Barabbas, and Mary Magdalene—who received the risen Lord? What did they have at stake? What was their relationship to Jesus and to one another? How are they related to us?

Carry on in Faith explores not only the well-known events that conclude Holy Week, but also the words and actions of Jesus, his disciples, and his enemies in the days leading up to the Last Supper. Some of the motivations and outcomes from that era are revealed. The reader is given a view of the apostolic community that emerged in the wake of Jesus' resurrection and ascension, and their reception of the Holy Spirit, sent by God to strengthen them.

The last days that Jesus' family, disciples, and friends were able to spend with him unfolded into a new way of life and became the first days with Jesus. When he told them to "do this and remember," Jesus was talking about taking the lessons he had given them, and with the guidance of the Holy Spirit of God becoming one like him. There is a challenge in the call to be like Jesus. Many already believe they could never do that, but so did his first disciples. He was the example of the humanity he expressed: a model for Christians for all of time.

As this intense human experience begins, the reader is asked to consume this book in bits and pieces. There are forty short daily readings and questions or comments for contemplation. Although the participant may consider the forty days during any season of the Church, especially during Lent or the Easter season, it is recommended that the readings begin twenty days before Easter and continue for twenty days after.

Reflecting Theologically

Theological reflection is a prayer and contemplation combination that involves the practitioner in a deeper understanding of our place with God and with each other. The purpose is to improve not only our faith life, but also how we navigate the day-to-day world. There are different methods and models for reflecting theologically, but here is the prescribed method for using this book in that way.

It is recommended that the reader take into consideration three things. Each chapter is a story in itself, and the reader should ask, first, how does each chapter relate to what he/she understands from the Bible? Would the society we live in today act any differently? Finally, ask the simple, "What would Jesus do?" but then also ask yourself, "What would I do?"

This is a book not just to read but to think about. Theological reflection asks the prayerful to consider how they experience Jesus in their lives, their culture and tradition, and the gospels, in an effort to always draw closer to the presence of God. In walking Jesus' last human days with him, we are meant to step into the light of a new life and begin every day with him, as the last becomes first.

Here are three simple steps:
1. Begin with prayer: "Lord, guide my senses, that I may experience sight, sound, and touch to imagine the fragrance and the flavor of your message for my life. Grant me your Holy Spirit to know the lesson you have for me, through Christ our Lord. Amen."
2. Read a chapter and contemplate the question(s) at the end.
3. Relax, sit in a comfortable position, with silence and dark or dim light. As you consider your understanding of the lesson, allow God's voice to enter your heart and mind, to express his understanding for your life. (Some may find it beneficial to repeat this process: to pray, read, and reflect theologically a second time.)

Sometimes meditation is a little unsettling to Catholics; it's not widely taught in the Church, but it should be an important component to our prayer. To pray is to speak to God; to meditate is to listen to him. It only requires one to relax the body and the thoughts of one's restless mind. Let the last days with Jesus become the first days of your new understanding in Christ.

Part I: The Last Days With Jesus

An Intense Human Experience

The real human experience of Christianity began in the last days of Jesus' mortal life during what is known today as the Triduum: the Lord's Supper on Holy Thursday, the passion on Good Friday, and the Easter Vigil (Holy Saturday). While these may have seemed like the last days with Jesus, they bled into the first days with him. Everything that took place during those three days was set in motion at the beginning of the week, a culmination of Jesus' intense human experience. Many smaller scenes turned out to be major events leading up to Jesus' death and resurrection, beginning with his appearance on what is known today as Palm Sunday. The gospels relay the experience; other writers have provided more of the details.

In the modern world we face an intense human experience like no other. Our nation has been in states of war, fighting around the globe, and squabbling at home. Nations have witnessed devastating earthquakes with increased violence, hurricanes rip cities from the ground, and man-made disasters push humanity to the limits. Our misuse and abuse of God-given resources, the planet itself, is becoming painfully obvious. Our institutions and trusted icons are threatened by scandals and sinfulness. What many are willing to render unto Caesar has become more than they are willing to render unto God.

This list of troubles could go on and on. These events parallel the times Jesus warned about during his last days. If we were told that our very lives depended on it, would we set aside time to walk with Christ as individuals and as a whole body, as the gospels call the faithful to do?

Jesus knew his own timetable and was preparing his spirit to move from being human to divine. Along the way, everyone who reached out to him was able to receive his touch in return. Jesus taught continuously. He prophesied of his own demise and resurrection and talked about good times and end times. Sometimes his words cut to the quick, but they were ever so true.

Q *Reflect on what you already know about the final week of Jesus' human life. How do you walk with Jesus today? Offer your prayers, works, joys, and sufferings for his intentions.*

To Touch the Hem of Jesus' Garment

At an earlier time, two unlikely believers reached out to Jesus on the same day and were touched by him in most powerful ways. These two incredible stories of faith appear in the same gospel reading because of their connection. Jesus was dealing with some of the most unique events of his ministry and had moved to the eastern side of the Sea of Galilee, to gentile territory under the dominion of Gerasa, and was immediately confronted by their demons, literally. The message—that faith in Jesus led to the kingdom of God, available to everyone, Jew or gentile—became a central theme in the gospels. Through faith in Jesus, anyone could be healed in mind and body. Up to that point in time, he had said very little about himself as the route to the Father, the source of all healing. Little did the world know that from that day on, he would be the Bread of Life, the Good Shepherd, the Light of the World, and the Vine. He would be all things to those in need of him.

After Jesus had again crossed the Sea of Galilee, he was back among the Jews, and a large crowd awaited him. Jairus was the "ruler" of a Jewish synagogue (which did not have rabbis as they would today). Some were very comparable to a mission church, "ruled" by a man who usually was a virtuous layperson, well-versed, well-educated, and acceptable to the community. Although the Gospel of Luke strongly indicates Jesus was returning to an area northwest of the sea, none of the three synoptic gospels names the place where Jairus lived.

Using a little official authority, the synagogue ruler made his way to the front, where Jesus was teaching, and knelt before him. He told the Lord that his daughter was near death, and he believed if Jesus would lay his hands on her, she would live. Moved by the man's great faith, Jesus accompanied him...as did the crowd. They were all pressing in, trying to get some sort of contact with the Messiah.

One of those people was a woman whose illness was not unlike leprosy, causing her to hemorrhage for twelve years. She had spent everything she had on cures, but to no avail. The Bible indicates she endured even greater suffering due to some of those healing attempts. She said, "If I could but touch the hem of his garment, I would be healed," and she managed to do just that. The bleeding and clotting dried up immediately, and she felt wellness taking hold.

Jesus seemed to be a little staggered by the drain of God's power as it flowed from him to cure the woman. He immediately acknowledged it, asking who touched him. The apostles told him it could have been anyone in such a huge crowd. The woman, realizing she had been found out, approached the Lord, trembling, and knelt at his feet. She told Jesus her whole story. He replied that her faith had saved her, and she could go in peace, cured of her affliction.

As this event was concluding, a messenger from Jairus' house arrived and reported that he need not bother the Master any further; the official's daughter had died. Jesus reassured the man and told him to just have faith, and they went on to his house. In those days, professional mourners were hired in advance of someone's death to mournfully lament and cry (keening), often covering themselves with sackcloth and ashes when the death was announced. This was the scene Jairus brought the Lord to. When Jesus told the group to stop, that the girl was not dead but only sleeping, they laughed and ridiculed him. Jesus had the house and yard cleared of all people but Jairus, his wife, and their family. Then, accompanied by his inner circle—the apostles Peter, James, and John—the Lord made his way to the girl's bedside. He took her hand, lifted his eyes to the Father, and told the twelve-year-old girl to rise. She did, walking around the place without affliction. The witnesses were utterly amazed. He instructed them to tell no one, but his request was not carried out.

Q *How have you or someone you know experienced the healing touch of the Father through Jesus' hand? Have you ever prayed for healing of mind or body?*

Lazarus' House

Only a few days before his triumphant ride into Jerusalem on what became known as Palm Sunday, Jesus had called on the Father to raise his friend, Lazarus, from a decomposing state of death to a living, healthy, and restored human being. Even though he had previously raised the young girl from death, this was easily his most amazing miracle to date. And by all accounts, it was witnessed by great numbers of believers and non-believers alike, and created a problem for Jesus' enemies. Pharisees, who feared Jesus' following was growing out of control, ran to the Sanhedrin to report and demand something be done to stop him. From that day on, Jesus was heavily escorted by his apostles, at Thomas' insistence.

A man named Caiaphas was the high priest that year, a title that gave him the authority of a prophet and freedom to say what he wanted. He prophesied that Jesus should not only die for the nation, but also that his death would serve to gather the children of God who were scattered abroad.

Knowing of the plot being formed against him, Jesus left Lazarus' home in Bethany and headed for the town of Ephraim, which bordered an extensive wilderness. While in Ephraim, Jesus privately taught the apostles many things. He reassured them of God's kingdom and revealed his passion, death, and resurrection to them again, with more urgency and bluntness than before. As time was drawing near for Passover, he made the choice to return to Jerusalem, circling around through Jericho, back to Bethany first.

Q *Jesus was not even safe in the home of his dearest friends, and he evaded his would-be captors, and even had doubts about fulfilling God's plan. Has fear ever kept you from doing God's will?*

Bartimaeus and Zacchaeus

On the trip to Jericho, Jesus gained notice again by curing Bartimaeus the blind beggar and sitting at table in the home of Zacchaeus the tax collector.

Bartimaeus the blind beggar represented the underside of Jericho. This was a city that may have already been nine thousand years old during Jesus' time. The people were above average in income and pride. At the same time, they had a large number of suffering and impoverished that they scarcely took care of. Bartimaeus represented that group.

When word came that Jesus and his companions were on their way there, it meant prosperity for the community and a chance to touch Jesus. It also meant that the lower classes of people needed to be hidden away, that the citizens not be embarrassed by the suffering and pain in their city. Bartimaeus was hidden from view, but that didn't quiet his voice. When he heard Jesus' band approaching, he began to cry out, "Jesus, Son of David, have mercy on me." Some of the crowd tried to silence him, but the blind man called out all the louder.

Finally, Jesus was near enough that he heard the voice among the commotion, and he asked that the beggar be brought to him. Disciples rounded up the blind man and told him to relax. He wasn't being carted away, but instead the Lord was calling for him to come forth. When Jesus asked what he wanted, Bartimaeus simply replied that he wanted to see. Jesus told him to go forth, that his faith had saved him, and the blind man was restored his sight. There was a new attitude in the crowd. Those who once spurned the beggar suddenly became friends of the friend of Jesus. Not only had the Lord restored his vision, but he also gave Bartimaeus a new opportunity.

On the other side of the coin were tax collectors. Jews who were employed by the Romans as tax collectors earned a specific hatred from the people. Publicans, as they were known, were in charge of taxing and turning the funds over to the Romans, but they were also allowed to charge extra fees and taxes and keep the money for themselves, so long as it did not become a riotous issue for the Romans. Zacchaeus was just such a man, serving the district of Jericho, where he was likely the most despised man in town. While Bartimaeus represented the lowly and suffering, Zacchaeus was rich and independent.

Aside from that, this publican was a man of small stature, which further caused him to be somewhat of a bully. He never hesitated to call on his guards to force his will on the people of Jericho. When he heard that Jesus was coming, he could have easily demanded the best seat in the house, but instead unassumingly climbed a tree so he could secretly see over the crowd and view the Lord as he passed by.

As fate would have it, Jesus walked right up to the tree where Zacchaeus clung, and he spoke up to him. The Messiah told the tax collector to come down because he was expecting to have dinner at his house that very night. It could be that Zacchaeus was one of the few people in town who could entertain a large party on short notice, and he immediately took responsibility to do so.

The crowd of reverent Jews gathered near Zacchaeus' home and complained to each other that Jesus had chosen to eat in the house of their hated enemy with the rest of his scurvy bunch. Inside, however, Jesus talked to the tax collector in a way he'd understand; he told the parable of the ten talents (coins). The story is about those who sit idly by, resting on their laurels rather than doing good deeds continuously. He told Zacchaeus and the others, for those who believe and continue their conversion, more will be given. "To everyone who has, more will be given, but from the one who has not, even what little he has will be taken away." His message was about continuing to do the best with whatever one has, growing in the faith.

The tax collector realized that Jesus was talking about the commandment to love God and care for one another, that the more one puts out for others, the greater their return will be in the kingdom of God; for he who shares what he has, more will be given to fulfill God's purpose. He repented of his crooked deals and proclaimed then and there that he would give half of what he owned to the poor. Further, Zacchaeus said he would do the right thing by those he had cheated in the past and return to them what he had taken and pay it back with interest. Jesus placed great value in the chief tax collector's repentance, blessed his house and praised his conversion. One undocumented legend is that Zacchaeus eventually became a bishop at Caesarea.

Q *Conversion to Jesus Christ is a day-to-day process. We are called to draw closer to the way, the truth, and the life in Jesus every day. Do you make an effort to grow in faith daily? What can you do to increase that effort?*

Palm Sunday

Six days before Passover, Jesus returned to Lazarus, Martha, and Mary in Bethany, and several true personalities emerged. Lazarus was the good friend and host; he reclined at table and chatted with Jesus. Mark's Gospel says this gathering took place in the home of Simon the Leper, who was probably one of those cured by Jesus. Mary, Lazarus' sister, used expensive ointment to anoint the feet of the Lord; her faith had become one of complete devotion. Martha, although she also served the Lord, became overwrought with the work ethic of being properly hospitable. Judas whined about wasting oil on Jesus' feet when it could have been sold for a handsome price and "given to the poor."

When word got out that Jesus was staying with his friends, the crowd returned, many more than before. They were not only there to see Jesus, but the miraculous Lazarus. In a likely attempt to avoid the crowd, the party had been taken to a place other than Lazarus' house. When the report reached the chief priests, planning began not only to arrest Jesus, but that Lazarus should also be put to death. His being alive was enough to stir Jesus' followers.

The next day, Jesus moved his base to Bethphage, a little village overlooking Jerusalem on the Mount of Olives (Mount Olivet, Jebel et-Tur). It was from there that he went on to make the triumphant entrance into Jerusalem, celebrated on Palm Sunday. There were already others working behind the scene to set up his final days, perhaps without even knowing what they were contributing to the story. Matthew reveals that Jesus dispatched two unnamed disciples to find a donkey and a colt tied up near the entrance to the village of Bethphage and to bring them back to him. There was even a secret code should anyone attempt to stop them. They were to respond to any question with the words, "The Lord has need of them," and they would be detained no further.

When Jesus rode into Jerusalem, the conversion he had brought to the people seemed obvious. They were strewing his path with the leaves of palm trees as they cheered, calling him the "Son of

David" (which would mean in their way of speaking that he was indeed the Messiah). Pharisees along the way were terribly upset by the adulation, and they insisted Jesus rebuke and silence the mob. He responded that if they were silent, even the stones would speak up in their place. God's word would not be silent. The chief priests were drawn to the fray because of the crowd and the growing belief.

Luke's Gospel tells that Jesus wept for the fate of the city before he entered it. From the place overlooking Jerusalem, he spoke in prayer, telling the populace they had missed the things that brought peace to the heart, that their opportunity to find these things through him was lost. He said their fate would be surrounded by their enemies and the city would be brought down even to the last stone. Popular opinion is that Jesus was speaking of the Roman invasion that destroyed the Temple and much of the city in AD 70, a thought that may be reconsidered when contemplating the history of the Jews and the conditions Israel lives with, even today.

Once in Jerusalem, Jesus went to the Temple and the crowds followed him. When people heard he was there, they came to him with every ailment and suffering. The priests were indignant to his healing in the Temple, and they also insisted that he silence the crowd and stop what he was doing. He rebuked the suggestion, which was just one step closer to sealing his fate.

The time had not come for him to be taken, so Jesus left Jerusalem that night and returned to Bethany. He was formulating the words and deeds, the prophecies, and the passion. Passover drew closer, and he wasn't going to stay away from Jerusalem for too long. What he revealed over those next few days is nothing short of incredible. As his time drew down to days and hours, the intensity of his message grew stronger.

> Q *Crowds would gather close to the Lord, many just to hear what he had to say. Others were sick or suffering. Each believed Jesus had a special message for their lives. Do you believe that Jesus has a special message for you? Relax, open your mind, and listen for it.*

Monday of Holy Week

Monday is the least celebrated day of Holy Week, and in our era, most of those gatherings are in the Episcopal and Orthodox Churches, two Christian faiths that have more than a passing similarity. It probably wasn't such a subdued occasion in the Lord's day.

On Sunday, Jesus had entered Jerusalem through the Golden Gate, which was directly before the Temple and held in Jewish tradition as the way the Messiah would enter the city. He was mobbed by friends and enemies. Jesus traveled back and forth from there through Bethphage to Bethany, remaining as incognito a traveler as his stature would allow, further delaying any attempt to arrest him. On Monday, Jesus sought solitude early before continuing his public ministry later. The signs of what was to come were beginning to wear on him, and his entrance into Jerusalem was quieter than the day before.

In one of his many works, *The Passion and Death of Jesus Christ*, Saint Alphonsus de Liguori tells a parable of a king, lord of many kingdoms, and his one and only, beautiful, holy, and wondrous son, who could not possibly have been loved more by his father. The young prince had affections for one of his slaves, who had been found guilty of a crime and sentenced to death. The prince offered himself in place of the slave. The king was vigilant in maintaining and guarding justice, and he accepted his son's condemnation that the slave might go free and escape the punishment well deserved. The son thus took on the role of malefactor for a crime he didn't commit, and the slave was freed.

Later in his book, the doctor of the Church agrees with two others, Saint Augustine, who said there is "nothing more conducive to the attainment of eternal salvation than to think every day of the pains which Jesus Christ suffered for the love of us," and Saint Bonaventure, "the wounds of Jesus are wounds which soften the hardest of hearts, and inflame the most frozen souls."

Even before the fact, Jesus was feeling his role in the parable

Liguori would one day tell. His passion inflamed frozen hearts but also kindled his staunchest enemies. He was on edge but remained focused on his mission. On Monday morning when he left Bethany, again headed to Jerusalem, he stopped at a fig tree, and finding it bare, condemned the plant and it withered in that moment. Even under the pressure, Jesus was still able to teach. The Lord informed observers, as he acted out his own parable, that as he had willed the tree to wither, so too could they who held their faith in the Father even move mountains. Jesus would tell his disciples, at the Last Supper, that some will not produce good fruit, and it is better that they are taken away so the healthier branches can.

Q *Since the beginning, God has given humanity dominion over the plants and the animals. The Old Testament Book of Leviticus even has planting instructions for farmers. Consider all the things we hear about the unhealthy care of our planet. Connectedness to all things is part of God's plan. Do you feel connected to other people? To other things?*

Cleansing the Temple

As with some of the other events of Holy Week, there is still a debate on exactly when the cleansing of the Temple took place. Sometimes the "when" is not as important as the "what." In Matthew's Gospel, it happened on the day Jesus entered Jerusalem, before he began to teach and heal there. John does not assign a chronology and includes it in the second chapter of his Gospel, well ahead of Holy Week. For Mark, it happened on Monday. What can be reasonably substantiated is that "something" happened in the Temple on Sunday before Jesus began to minister there. It is entirely possible that Jesus and the apostles had to struggle to acquire his "spot" in the Temple every day he went. Some came to hear his words, others wanted miracles, but still others didn't want him there at all. The Lord returned to Jerusalem from Bethphage on the Mount of Olives to continue teaching and healing every day of Holy Week until he was finally stopped.

The story of the Temple cleansing is an indication of Jesus' ongoing frustration with what had become of the faith of the people. He reacted in kind to a decline in holiness by the thievery and marketing that took place in the house of prayer, and how he had watched it get worse and worse every year of his life. Passover had become like a bazaar, profited from and sponsored by the very same people who sought to condemn him. Attacking their commerce could not be tolerated.

The Temple was laid out in layers. The Sanhedrin, the priests, and the upper-class Jewish men were permitted to go the furthest inside. The layers extended out dividing the worshipers by race, gender, social class, and age. On the outside, in a courtyard of the Temple, booths were set up. Holocaust offerings were sold at a premium price, and rumor had it that one could buy pleasures of the flesh, food, clothing, and more, anything needed by the vast throng of pilgrims. Jesus couldn't stand the disrespect and dishonesty of the sellers any longer. Accompanied by some of the disciples, he attacked the moneychangers, spilling their coins on the ground near the feet of beggars, and released their holocaust offerings to run off or fly away. When order was restored, there were many whispers, but also silence. Jesus was already inside the Temple.

One of the groups that clamored to see Jesus was a band of gentiles, mostly Greeks who had come to Jerusalem to worship during the Passover. They found Philip, the apostle from Bethsaida, one of their people, and asked to see Jesus. Philip deferred to Andrew, who told Jesus, and all those in the presence of the Lord heard one of his finest orations.

He told Andrew and Philip that the hour had come for his glorification, meaning his arrest was looming. To the crowd, he said that unless a grain of wheat falls to the ground and dies, a grain of wheat is all it will ever be, but if that grain dies, it becomes a plant producing much fruit. Like the proverb, if one truly desires eternal life in God, he must be willing to die to the things in worldly life. Philip understood, as he had reportedly been a man of means who left it to follow Jesus.

Jesus admitted to his exasperation, and asked, "What am I supposed to say: Father, save me from this hour?" His passion was the purpose for which he came. He prayed to the Father, "Glorify your name." At that moment a sound filled the halls of the Temple. Some witnesses tried to dismiss it as thunder and others thought an angel spoke to Jesus. It was the Father who said, "I have glorified it and will again," in a voice that obviously wasn't audible to everyone.

Jesus said that the time of judgment was being carried out. He said this would be condemnation of the evil that ruled in the world, and the Savior would die and be raised up, offering to draw all along with him. There were scoffers among them, and some challenged him to reveal the true Son of Man. He instructed them to walk in "the light," that darkness may not overcome them; if one walks in darkness he will not find the way. Monday before dusk, after telling them these things, Jesus slipped away and returned to the Mount of Olives.

Q *Light is the symbol of the Lord. It is the first thing God created in the story of creation. Jesus tells us to walk in light, not darkness. What things have helped you stay on the lighted path to Jesus today? What has made it easier to stray into darkness?*

Teaching Tuesday

It was still dark early Tuesday morning when Jesus set out for the Temple in Jerusalem. The timetable was accelerating, and there was still much to be done. Passover drew closer, and as they still do today, Jewish pilgrims had arrived and were continuing to arrive in Jerusalem. Some had heard about Jesus, and they sought him in the Temple. At the withered fig tree, Jesus told his followers that the key to prayer was faith; if one truly believed in what they asked of the Father, it would be granted them, and whenever one prays, he should also offer forgiveness and hold no grudge, that the Father will bestow the same mercy on him. Complete faith cures doubt.

Jesus arrived with his entourage at the Temple and was met by the chief priests and elders. They blocked his path, demanding to know who gave him authority to do what he was doing in the Temple. Jesus told them he would answer the question if they would first answer one of his. He asked them where baptism by John originated, in heaven or by human hand. They discussed it among themselves, determining that if they said heaven, Jesus would ask why they didn't believe the baptizer, and if they said by human origin, the crowd who revered John as a prophet would turn on them. So they simply told Jesus they didn't know. He replied, "Neither shall I tell you by what authority I do these things."

Before they could slink away, Jesus relayed a parable to the priests and elders. He said a man had two sons, both of whom he asked to work in the vineyard. One said no, but repented later and went to work. The other said he would and never showed up in the vineyard. Jesus asked which of the two did the will of the father. The crowd quickly agreed that it was the first one, who actually did the work even though he previously had said he would not. Jesus told the priests and elders that harlots and tax collectors would go to the kingdom of heaven before them. He said, while the lofty did not believe John, who came to them in righteousness, those they called sinners did. "Even now," Jesus told them, "You do not repent and believe."

The Jewish leaders were still searching for a dignified exit when Jesus said to them, "hear another parable." He told them about a landowner who built a fabulous "green" business, where the entire vine-growing and winemaking process could take place all at one locale, and he leased it to be operated by the tenants. Then he moved away. After the harvest, he sent servants to collect his share. Instead, the tenants beat them and stoned them until the servants were dead. A second and larger contingent met the same fate. A third was led by the landowner's son, and when the tenants saw him, they thought they could kill him and seize ownership of the property. Jesus asked the group what they suspected the owner would do when he came. The unanimous answer was that he would inflict a miserable death on them and lease the land to new tenants.

The Teacher quoted to the crowd from the 118th Psalm, "The stone which the builders rejected has become the cornerstone. It has been done by the LORD and is marvelous in our eyes." He told them that, like the tenants, this and the kingdom of heaven could all be taken away from them, and they could be crushed by the very cornerstone they rejected. When they realized he was talking about them, the leaders considered arresting him on the spot but feared the mob and did not do so.

Jesus continued to teach and cure throughout the day. A group of Sadducees, who differed from Pharisees in part because they did not believe in an afterlife or a coming Messiah, came to him and revealed their lack of understanding by posing ridiculous questions about those subjects. Jesus knew they were asking questions about things they did not believe in, and he responded to them that they neither knew Scripture or the power of God. It was then that a scribe approached and asked him, "What is the greatest commandment?" Jesus reaffirmed a teaching that had existed further back than the texts of the ancient Hebrews. Jesus had spoken the answer before, as well. Love God with all your heart, soul, and mind, and show that love by the way you care for one another. The gospels say the inquisitor understood Jesus' teaching, to which the Teacher reassured him: He was near the kingdom of God.

After that, the petty questioning ended. Jesus called out to the Pharisees, asking them who they thought the Messiah was, to which they responded—as was their traditional belief—that the Messiah was the son of David. Jesus responded with another question, asking why then did David call him Lord. From then on, the questions from those in authority became fewer.

By the afternoon, all sorts of characters were gathered: Sadducees, Pharisees, scribes, Greeks, ranking officials, and ordinary folk. Jesus addressed the crowd and told them the priests took the seat of Moses and are honest in delivering the law, but not as practitioners of it (he basically told them, do what they say, not what they do). He challenged the leaders' lack of humility and their public display of "righteousness." The Lord used harsh words against those who falsified their acts of faith and those who sat as judges and protectors of the law held over others, using the very words of the Mosaic law that they abused. He condemned not only the crime of their forefathers and ancestors in killing the prophets, the messengers of God, but the fact they proclaimed their righteousness by saying they would never have allowed something like that to happen on their watch. Only Jesus knew that they were about to do it again by taking him to his torture and death.

All day long, Jesus had seen the pilgrims bring their offerings to the coffers of the Temple. When a poor woman, clothed in rags, came in and deposited both of the small copper coins she had, he was moved to speak. He chastised the rich who came in and gave from what was left over after their huge profits and praised the woman who gave everything from her poverty.

Q *The greatest commandment is the essential rule of the covenant with God. We are always called to think of others before ourselves. How have you been willing to give to others from what you have? Have you given your best or your least?*

Tuesday Night and the Eschatological Discourse

It was getting near dusk on Tuesday, and Jesus had been healing the sick and teaching the throngs that had gathered in the Temple all day long. It became more dangerous in the city after dark, and Jesus returned to Bethphage. As they left the Temple, Jesus saw his apostles dallying and admiring the grace and beauty of the Temple architecture, and told them, "Of all these things there will not be left one stone upon another."

The group moved in silence and even passed the withered fig tree on the road. Finally they came to a place on the mountain where they sat before the sunset that blazoned across the Temple exterior in the distance, as it sat more than 150 feet lower than the mountaintop. Perhaps the apostles all had the same question in mind, but no one spoke of it. At last, Jesus sat near Peter, James, John, and Andrew. They asked him to speak plainly and tell them what he meant about the destruction of the Temple. Would there be signs and when will it happen?

The Teacher told his closest followers to be sure they were not deceived because others would come in the name of the Messiah, but they would be deceivers. Before the end, he warned there would be wars and rumors of wars, and as frightening as they may be, "the end is not yet." The Lord's followers will be hunted and persecuted, hated in every nation because of Jesus' name. Many who followed will become sinful enemies of the faith and of each other. They will be deceived by false prophets and wrong teachings. Evildoings will so permeate the world that love will grow cold in the hearts of many. The one who perseveres to the end will be saved. The gospel of the kingdom will be preached throughout the world that all nations may come to it, and then the end will come. In essence he told them they would have to endure a hailstorm of suffering before the promised glory of the Messiah returns to earth. The Church itself will be rocked by attacks from within as well as from the outside.

Jesus used words from the Book of Daniel to define the "desolate abomination" of the holy place. The Old Testament book referred to desecration of the Temple and a military presence within its walls. Jesus gave a warning that was similar to the one shared with Lot and his family at Sodom: Run for the hills and don't look back, and do not be blinded by the sight of pseudo-messiahs. Do not anyone be fooled by false hopes and promises from prophets and miracle workers, as even the religious will be susceptible to their words, and do not be deceived with stories and apparitions, because the real Messiah will be as visible as lightning in the sky when he returns... there will be no doubt.

In those days following the tribulation, the sun and moon will be dark, and stars will fall from the sky. The powers of heaven will be shaken. Then and only then will there be a sign of the Son of Man, who will return in power and glory as he departed: on a cloud. When this concept appeared earlier in the Book of Daniel, the author spoke of the arrival of Michael the Archangel, guardian of the people, and that everyone whose name is "written in the book" will be saved; Jesus said they would be gathered by the angels from the corners of the world.

Only the Father knows when this will be, he told them. Some will not recognize what is happening, and like the people of Noah's era, they will continue in their revelry and ignorance until they are swept away. Many will simply become bogged down by their attachment to this earthly life. People standing together will not be guaranteed safety; one will be taken away and the other, not. And he said to be prepared for him always. He asked who knows when the thief will come in the night (or if it even be night), for surely if he did, he would only be on guard at that designated time.

Through a series of parables, appearing primarily in the twenty-fifth chapter of Matthew, which is entirely composed of Jesus' oration, he taught that no one who is a true servant will take command over others and treat them as beneath him/herself, that people should not be misled into placing their set of values in the wrong place, so they do not wake up outside when the door has already been closed.

Jesus retold the parable of the talents, reminding his apostles that humans are not to rest on their achievements and past laurels, that they are to build on their faith with understanding and practice. People never find life in Christ by burying what they have in the sand, assuming it is enough. This is certainly a reference to true conversion in Jesus Christ, which all are told is an ongoing process.

When the Son of Man returns to his throne, he will call forth every nation and will separate them like sheep and goats. "Come, those who are blessed by my Father to inherit the kingdom he has prepared for you since the beginning of the world." He told them, those who were saved fed him when he was hungry, gave him drink when he was thirsty, welcomed him when he was a stranger, clothed him when he was naked, cared for him when he was infirmed, and visited him in prison. The others will be shuffled off to the eternal fire of a place prepared for Satan and his angels. The apostles reminded Jesus that they had not done one of those things for him, and he told them that anytime they did those things for the suffering, the least of his, they did it for him, and they will have eternal life.

Q *Jesus emphasized caring for one another throughout his earthly ministry as a means to express our love for God. Contemplate the things you do for others, and if you do not already minister in this way, plan a time when you will involve yourself in this holy service.*

The Petition to Arrest Jesus

Jesus alerted the apostles to the fact that Passover was only two days away, and he would then be handed over to the chief priests to be crucified. At that same time the priests and elders were meeting in Jerusalem at the palace of the high priest, Caiaphas. Several times before, the Sanhedrin had called for Jesus to be arrested and stopped from his deeds, but never before had a vote been taken that resulted in a decision to bring an end to Jesus' ministry, no matter what the cost. Some members of the governing body were silent followers of Jesus and would serve him later, but the vote taken that night, near midnight, following much debate, was unanimous. Officers were told the following morning to arrest him, but not in public.

Although the vote was a knee-jerk reaction of the priests and elders to the accusations and condemnations Jesus proclaimed in the Temple that day, the plot had been brewing for some time. They believed he wouldn't return to the Temple on Wednesday, so the Sanhedrin began to craft a plan whereby the Lord could be arrested Thursday night, away from the festivities of Passover.

It was near midnight on Tuesday when the Sanhedrin completed its clandestine mission. A plan was formed, calling for the death of Jesus Christ. The priests and elders slipped off into the night, agreeing to meet midmorning of the next day to draw up articles for Jesus' arrest. It was the day before Passover and the feast of the Unleavened Bread.

On Tuesday, when Jesus was teaching in the Temple, Judas Iscariot, one of the twelve apostles, was dining with relatives who were Sadducees. Among them was Annas, a member of the Sanhedrin, a retired high priest. Somewhere in the conversation the retired priest let it slip that the Sanhedrin was meeting in secret that night to determine the fate of Jesus. He made comments that suggested to Judas there would be honor in helping bring in this enemy of Rome and of Israel. Judas saw it as an opportunity to force Jesus' hand and start the revolution to drive the Romans out of all Palestine. Surely the Lord and his followers would never allow him to be arrested or punished. The Jewish officials were in need of someone who knew Jesus' movements and could readily identify him in a crowd.

Q *God always knew what Judas' role would be. Even when we choose the wrong reasons, the Father can make his good will come of them. Do you try to do things with good and positive reasoning? Do you keep in mind trying to do what Jesus would do?*

Judas and the Sanhedrin

Judas Iscariot was a Maccabean raised in a military regimen. His father and grandfather were warriors, having fought against Rome. Judas was expected to take up the banner, but instead, as the male heir to the family estate, he stayed at home, caring for his father's land and his mother and sister.

He did remain active with other Zealots who sought to overthrow the Romans. If, as some scholars suppose, the designation "Iscariot" was translated from the Greek word "sikarios," he was thus Judas the assassin. At least for a time, he belonged to an extremist group of Zealots who were planning an uprising. He was likely a follower of Barabbas, who was an extremely violent revolutionary and leader of a band of terrorists. That renegade ascended to prominence just a few days before Passover, when he was accused of inciting a riot and killing someone. It has often been supposed that his victim was a Roman centurion, which is unlikely considering the rebel's fate on Good Friday; the Romans would not have permitted his release if he had murdered one of their own.

In the beginning, Judas was as important as anyone else among the apostles. According to John, he was the treasurer. Despite misaligned values from time to time, he is known to have carried money and goods from the disciples to the poor. Although John also refers to him as a devil and a thief, those incidents are generally dismissed as the evangelist's reaction to some other stimulus rather than fact.

Judas was not the warrior his father and grandfather were—and certainly no Barabbas—but he dreamt of the fall of Roman rule and had illusions of how he might help bring that about. When he heard what Annas had to say on Tuesday, Judas pictured a situation where he couldn't lose. First, he would be recognized for his heroics in bringing Jesus to justice. Second, the Messiah would never permit himself to be killed, and he would rise up to lead the Jews over the Romans. Judas had not lost his faith in Jesus, only in the peaceful way the Lord approached everything. When he saw how Jesus could stir things up in the Temple, he was reignited to believe he could be the military Messiah, who one segment of Zealots had so long awaited.

There was no mention of money when Judas met his relatives and Annas on Tuesday, and there was no mention of money when he went to the Sanhedrin who were meeting at Caiaphas' palace on Wednesday morning. Sadducees, those who held the Torah as the only law and did not believe in immortality of the soul or resurrection of the body, were the dominant party, but there were also the Pharisees who did believe in those things and also taught of God's love for every individual. Rather than complete reliance on the Torah, they advocated an oral tradition of passing on ancient and modern wisdom.

Both groups wanted to do away with Jesus, but for different reasons and by different methods. The foremost Sadducee was Caiaphas himself, and he proposed that Jesus simply be assassinated. The Pharisees were opposed to the way Jesus berated them and their hold on the people, but it was his attack in the Temple that pushed them over the edge. Still, they would not condone the assassination plot and pushed for arrest and trial. When that was the decision everyone agreed to, Judas offered his services to locate Jesus for them. He would thus be cast for all ages as a traitor; even his name is synonymous with betrayal. Jesus knew all of this when he selected Judas.

The first days of Holy Week offer a multitude of opportunities for the modern-day faithful to celebrate reconciliation. All Christian churches provide some type of penitential service: Stations of the Cross, Tenebrae, and services for the sick, which includes those who are sick in the soul. One can hardly imagine what might have gone through Judas' mind as he wavered back and forth from Tuesday through Thursday, thinking "yes," then "no," not unlike many of the challenges Christians inwardly debate today. The temptation to make the wrong choice continues to assault no matter how frequently it is rebuked.

Q *Do you have issues that are hard to decide, causing you to change your mind back and forth? It is in prayer (speaking to God) and meditation (listening to God) that we begin to understand his plan for everything. How often do you simply pray and believe in God's way and let that be your choice?*

Holy Thursday of the Lord's Supper

On the Mount of Olives, Jesus spent Wednesday in prayer and meditation. The time was getting near, and everything had been set in motion according to God's plan. The Lord and his followers moved down the hill, closer to the city, and made camp at a place near Gethsemane.

It was unfathomable that witnesses to his teaching and some of those who had seen the miracles and signs did not believe. Jesus knew but still had to deal with it on the painful human level. He quoted from Isaiah, telling his disciples, "Who would believe what we have heard? To whom has the arm of the Lord been revealed?" and "Listen carefully, but you shall not understand. Look intently, but you will know nothing." Even then, there were many among the Jews who believed in him but hid from the truth in fear of expulsion from the Temple. Jesus reminded them that his words were not his alone but those of the Father in whose name Jesus had come, not to judge the world but to save it.

In Jerusalem, as night fell, there was cleaning and cooking. Prayer and worship were being planned. Everything was made to order for the celebration of the holy feast. Moneychangers and their livestock were returned to the Temple. Jesus contemplated, not in days, but in hours.

Jerusalem is normally known for a dry, arid climate in late spring. The day of the feast was a day of calm, balmy weather; it got cold overnight. Throughout the modern Christian world, celebrations recall the institution of the Eucharist at the Last Supper. Although questions persist about the exact day and hour every event took place, Passover was underway. The date on the Hebrew calendar was Nisan 14, in a year believed to be AD 30, according to the Julian calendar. Jews from all over the known world had come to Jerusalem for the celebration, and many of those locals who would become Christians enjoyed the festival right alongside them. The first day of the feast of the Unleavened Bread was about to initiate a change that would affect the entire world forever. That day, among those people gathered, was the beginning of the Christian character...an intense human experience.

Q *Even today, not only practitioners of Judaism, but people of all faiths gather to honor their expression of divinity and their tradition. How do you celebrate the days of our salvation through Jesus? Do you set aside time to walk with him in some way on Holy Thursday, Good Friday, and/or Holy Saturday?*

The First Eucharist

The days of the Jewish faith begin at sundown, and so does Passover. Throngs of people milled about through the bazaars and exhibits that lined the streets of Jerusalem during the day and filed in and out of the Temple. There were many Greeks including the estimated thirty that met Jesus in the Temple. There were literally people from every accessible country around the Mediterranean, from the European continent to Asia Minor and North Africa.

The Passover meal comes on the first day of the celebration, and it is not until the next day that the feast of the Unleavened Bread takes place. Some texts indicate that the Last Supper took place on the feast day, while others insist it was during the Passover meal, as has been previously mentioned. There is also a scholarly endeavor, based on John's Gospel, that suggests it wasn't Passover yet, and Jesus died before it began. The exact date when the Last Supper took place is a trivial pursuit when compared to the depth and importance of the message.

One event that the synoptic gospels agree on is that preparation for a meal took place during the day on Thursday. Matthew, Mark, and Luke all say it was the day of the feast of the Unleavened Bread and the day for sacrificing the Passover lamb. This is another symbol of ancient Hebrew roots; the lamb of God was named during the Exodus, long before Jesus was on earth. For Christians today, this was the night Jesus became the Lamb of God.

Peter and John asked him where he wanted to prepare for the feast. Jesus told them to go into the city where a man carrying a jar of water would secretly meet them. There was a gate into the city known as the Essene gate, located on the back side of the city near where the "upper room" was. There, they met the stranger, who led the two apostles through the back streets and around the corners of Jerusalem until he presented them at his Master's house. Peter and John addressed the homeowner as the Lord had taught them: "The Teacher says to you, 'where is the guest room that I may eat the Passover with my disciples?'" He took them to a large upper room that was furnished for the occasion and left them to prepare the celebration.

Pilgrims in Jerusalem today can see what is/was the upper room. The building is located near the Dormition Abbey outside the modern city walls. It is on a mound known at various times as Mount Zion or the Western Hill, both of which may be misnomers. The room there today is built precisely over the grave of King David, separated from his tomb by ruins that may have been the original chamber. The upper room was at some time destroyed but reconstructed by the Crusaders in the fourteenth century. The location can be reasonably presumed accurate.

Another twist at this point: Matthew and Mark tell the story of Jesus being anointed with oil at Simon the Leper's house in Bethany right before the telling of the Last Supper, and both evangelists include a serious chastising of Judas by the Lord. It is perhaps intended to show part of the reason for Judas' betrayal, and although it had actually taken place in the days before Holy Week, it apparently continued to irritate the betrayer.

Also interesting is the question of when Jesus acknowledged that there was a betrayer among them. Luke says the announcement came after the institution of the paschal feast, while Mark and Matthew list it before the sacramental moment. None of the three ever say that Judas was dismissed without sharing in the Last Supper, the institution of the Eucharist.

Q *Imagine you are the host/hostess for a religious celebration honoring the presence of the Lord. You have spent time with him and heard his words. What would you do to make the feast appropriate and comfortable for Jesus and his guests? When you honor visitors in your home, do you prepare for them in a way that shows your gratitude for their presence? Do you invite Jesus into your home?*

Jesus Serves His Followers

When Jesus walked into the upper chamber that night, everyone was already at the tables, which in those days, would have been round or in a u-shape, not like the famous rectangle depiction created by Leonardo da Vinci. The idea was to lie down to eat, one's head at the table and their feet sticking out from the other end of a cot. There was a minimum of three tables in the upper room to accommodate the followers who had gathered with the Lord, although one was certainly reserved for Jesus and his chosen twelve.

A reason for this kind of seating, intended for the guests' comfort, is because of the care given to feet in those days. Simply put, feet were nasty. There weren't cars or buses, not even bicycles. The inability to walk could be fatal, and thus the health and grooming of feet was very important. A servant, whose specialty was to go around the table and wash the guests' feet as they ate, would enter and tend to the task. This was the lowest form of servitude, but it was a specialty and could not be designated to just anyone.

The Lord shared with them the customary wine "toast" and expressed his joy at being able to share his last meal with them before his suffering. He told the disciples: Indeed, he would not again drink the fruit of the vine with them until the coming of the Father's kingdom.

Then Jesus removed his outer tunic and began the role of the servants, washing and anointing the feet of his closest friends. This caused great concern among the apostles who did not wish him to serve them this way. He asked if they understood what he was doing. Jesus taught the value of personal service by everyone, even by the Son of God.

The first Eucharist was a wonderful expression that has been the foundation of faith commemorated in Christian churches ever since. During it, Jesus spoke of the connection between all things and God. Service for others illustrated an equally important part of Christian life as the Eucharist itself. As James would later write, "Faith of itself without works is dead," assuring his audience that works are the demonstration of one's faith. Jesus told them that in order to be first, they must be last.

According to John's Gospel, during the meal, while they were reclining, Jesus announced that there was a betrayer among them. They all wanted to know who, each begging that he be removed from the list of suspects. Jesus said the betrayer would dip his hand in the dish with him, but by that time, they'd all reached into the bowl. Jesus told John secretly that he would indicate who by handing that person a morsel of the bitter herb, maror, which he dipped in charoset, a spicy fruit, nut, and wine concoction. In the ensuing conversations, the apostles were rattled. Even the ones who saw Jesus pass the sign on to Judas, who promptly left the chamber, assumed that the two men were conducting regular business. The apostles argued among themselves, not only about who might be the traitor, but also who might be the greatest among them. To Jesus, it must have seemed they missed the point altogether.

Then he took the bread. Jesus gave thanks to the Father, blessed the bread, broke it, gave it to all of them, and told them, "This is my body; take it and eat." He also took the cup of wine and told them it was his blood of a new covenant, that it would be shed for them and for all. Jesus told them to always do this and remember. No one immediately understood that he was telling them to take of himself, the Bread of Life, to take of his ways, become one with the presence of God, and to become servants all to one another.

The three synoptic gospels focus on this institution of the blessed Eucharist. John's Gospel reports: Jesus used the entire evening to teach the disciples, and the wisdom he passed on filled four chapters of the gospel. Every life-in-Christ lesson there ever was can be found in those last discourses.

Q *Think of a time you did something sacrificial for another person. Did you feel joy in performing the service? Do you feel that caring for others is a natural thing for people to do willingly? Would you continue to care for others if it involved great sacrifice?*

The Last Discourses

After Judas was gone, the Lord announced that the prophecy was happening, that he had been glorified and, therefore, God had been glorified through him. What other important things could Jesus possibly tell his disciples on that Holy Thursday evening? They were all gathered, had shared the Passover feast, been witnesses to the institution of the Holy Eucharist, and were ready to be filled one last time with his words. Jesus gathered with his friends. He knew there was only a little while. In essence, he gave them the life lesson, a summary of all the teaching of his ministry.

The Teacher started by telling the disciples there was a new commandment: Love one another. He said, "As I have loved you, so also should you love one another. This is how all will know you are my disciples, if you have love for one another." You could've heard a pin drop in the room. He had told them about love before, but this was about being one people in Christ. It was like Saint Francis instructing to "preach the gospel always, and if needed, use words." On that night, our Lord created the priesthood with a promise and commitment for future generations.

Because he said so, it should come as no surprise that there have been cracks in that foundation. Just a few days before the Last Supper, while sitting with the apostles, he told of a time when the Church would be attacked from within and from the outside. The Church has always been a work in progress, not yet perfected. One recent indiscretion suggests that in the wake of the Second Vatican Council, and facing a shortage of priests, the Church allowed men to enter the priesthood who shouldn't have. For whatever reason it happened, there must be reparation among the Catholic people themselves to continue the work in progress. The longer it takes to resolve and forgive, the more strain it puts on the Church and its very meaning. On May 1, 2011, when Pope John Paul II was beatified in Rome, protesters, some of whom were victims of priests' abuse, demonstrated in the United States, claiming he should not be canonized because it was ignoring the victims under his watch. There have been some very holy priests over the two millennia of the Church such as Peter Claver, Vincent De Paul, John Bosco, John of the Cross, Saint Jerome—and many, many more—some of whose names aren't even known. Of course, there were some bad ones, too.

Not all of the first disciples ordained to carry on Jesus' mission were men. Joanna, Susanna, Salome, and Mary Magdalene—apostle to the apostles—stood among the ordained. In the first generation of Christians after Christ's resurrection, many other women rose to religious orders and leadership.

Knowing there would be trouble in the priesthood from time to time, Jesus immediately pointed to the failings of his first priest, bishop, and pope, Peter. When he told Peter that he would deny the Lord three times overnight, the apostle was outraged. Jesus wasn't just talking about him alone, since they all ran and hid, all but John, who was present at the crucifixion. He was acknowledging the times anyone might hide from God.

Jesus told them he knew they had faith in the Father and that they should also have faith in him. He told them of his wish that where he was going, so too, they would also be, to which Thomas replied, the apostles didn't know the way. Jesus told him they did know the way, and the truth, and the life...and it was Christ. "If you know me then you'll also know the Father." Philip asked Jesus to show them the Father, asserting that would be all the proof they needed. Jesus, in response, asked if they had spent all that time together, and he still didn't realize that when he saw Jesus he saw the Father. "Do you not believe that I am in the Father, and the Father is in me?" He said his words and works were the Father working through him, a reminder that we are all called as a people to let God work through us. Jesus told the apostles he was going to the Father and would support them there, that greater things than he had done were yet to come.

Q *What is done in Jesus' name will be fulfilled, and sin is not something done in the name of Christ. Even though we try, sometimes we deny Christ by the actions we do. Think of a recent time you denied Christ by committing a sinful act that you knew was wrong.*

The Advocate

One of the most revealing parts of his speech was about the Advocate, the Holy Spirit, whom he would pray to the Father for the disciples to receive. Jesus said this Holy Spirit would live within them, that the Holy Spirit is truth. He told them the truth was something the whole world didn't see or know and therefore didn't accept. "I will not leave you orphans," he said. Jesus' life beyond this one was something that not all would ever see, but he would be alive in the hearts and minds of those who believe in him. Agapé love would be handed down by the Father to those who keep his commandments, and love would be returned to the Father by those who are faithful. He distinguished that there would be people who would not love him or the Father, nor believe in his resurrection, and therefore not believe in the Church which he set forth. Jesus told them the Advocate knows the answer to all things and would reveal them to those who accept him in their hearts and minds. The Holy Spirit would remind them of all that Jesus said and did.

"Peace I leave with you; my peace I give to you." The peace Jesus spoke of is not the worldly kind one might imagine, but inner peace with God. In truth, he was telling them to persevere no matter how many stand against them. If God's love is really alive in someone, then he will find peace of mind even in the darkest hour. The faithful would suffer, but they should recall that Jesus suffered for them first, and the way of the Lord will be triumphant. "Rejoice that I go to the Father, for he is greater than I." He told them of these things before they happened, that when they did, at last, his followers would believe.

Jesus revealed the secrets of the vine, the meaning of which has been diluted by time. Most people don't have vineyards in modern days and may not understand the nurturing of the vine grower. This was an allusion to how the persons of the Holy Trinity care and maintain the human life that lives in love and dignity. He told of the ultimate care given to the vines that they might produce abundant fruit, while some unhealthy branches are trimmed away so others might live. Without taking in all of the right elements, the branches do not thrive as they were meant to. The Son is the vine from which all good things come. The Father, the vine dresser, would raise each branch to be its best. The Holy Spirit would be like the sun and the rain offering everything needed to grow in the loving presence of God.

The Lord assured them that they would have friends, but their enemies would be in great number, too. These are the people who are guided by evil intent. They did not love God, and they will not love God in the days to come. "I will come to you," He told them. He instructed them to be strong in the sight of the Holy Trinity, even if they are surrounded by those who don't believe.

As the disciples disbanded, some followed Jesus, believing they were heading back to the Mount of the Olives. The small band descended the stone pathway, crossed the Valley of Kedron, and passed by the Garden of Gethsemane, which was near the Golden Gate of Jerusalem. Jesus stopped to pray, and he chose Peter, James, and John to remain closest to him while he did. In his final words to all of them he said, "In a little while you will no longer see me; then you will one day see me again."

Q *Think of the image of the vine and branches: the Son is a vine giving life and nutrition to the souls of branches, the Father as ever-present vine dresser, nurturing and caring for the branches, and the Holy Spirit that brings sun and rain, the spirit with which the branches come to life. Contemplate your part as a branch in the connectedness of all things.*

The Longest Day There Ever Was

Even though Jesus had told them so, the apostles didn't immediately realize they were heading into a night and day that would seem to last forever, opening the door to a time that would be filled with only darkness and uncertainty. After Jesus finished his Last Supper discourses, the apostles told him that they finally understood, and they believed he knew all things. They said no one should have to question him to know that he came from God. Jesus double-checked by asking again if they finally believed and answered his own question by telling his followers the hour was coming when they would run off to hide, leaving him, but he would not be alone, because the Father was with him.

Before they left the upper room, Jesus prayed. He asked his Father to give him glory that he may in turn give the glory back to the Father. He was born to make it possible for all to have eternal life and had been entrusted with that mission. He had succeeded by revealing and glorifying the name of God before them. Jesus prayed to reaffirm his position with the Father. He prayed for his disciples and for the future and well-being of the Church.

Most of the group disbanded for the night, and the others escorted Jesus as he left the city. When he stopped again to pray near the Garden of Gethsemane, Jesus knew he would not be leaving in their company. He took Peter, James, and John with him and went to what archeological finds have discovered was a cave, not in the garden, but adjoining it. Two thousand years ago, that cave was probably more of a grotto, where one could enter and pray privately. The three apostles were supposed to watch outside while Jesus went in. Very few eyes would be witness to when the Pharisee's armed guards would show up.

Jesus prostrated himself and prayed that the "cup" of what he was about to drink be taken from him, but he moved beyond that to an expression of acceptance and obedience to God's will. Then he went to see if anything had happened yet and found the three apostles asleep. Jesus scolded them for not staying awake with him and instructed the three to watch and pray that they wouldn't succumb to temptation.

Jesus returned to the grotto and expressed having overcome his doubt and rededicated himself to finishing what he had been sent to do. He checked on the apostles who were sleeping again, but he left them there and finished his prayer. For the third time, he pledged himself to the mission, and an angel appeared before him to provide Jesus the strength sent by the Father, that he would be able to endure this greatest sacrifice. He prayed even more feverishly, and his sweat became like drops of blood falling to the ground.

When the prayer was done, Jesus returned to the three apostles and asked them rhetorically if they were still sleeping. They all jumped up from their slumber to a heightened state of alertness. He told them the time had come, and they should all go to meet the betrayer. They stepped out into the path leading back through the garden, which would also be the direction they would take if going back to the Mount of Olives. As he predicted, there was Judas, waiting with the guards, and he confirmed which one was Jesus by kissing the Lord's cheek. Historical indicators suggest the other apostles still didn't all know Judas was the betrayer until that moment, except John, who knew because Jesus had given him a sign after sharing secret, whispered information at the supper table.

Eyewitnesses do not all agree on exactly what happened next. According to John, when Jesus crossed the Kedron Valley to the garden, he deliberately went to a place Judas also knew, but that he approached the soldiers and the betrayer, rather than the other way around. When he did, they asked the whereabouts of Jesus the Nazorean and were frightened because he identified himself, using the name of God which was given to Moses. The crowd had grown by that time with friends and enemies. When approached by Judas, Matthew says Jesus called him friend and told him to get on with what he had to do, while Luke testifies that Jesus questioned him as to whether he was coming to betray the Son of Man with a kiss.

There was certainly a moment that could have turned into a riot had his followers not been calmed by Jesus, as he reminded them, these events must happen to fulfill the prophecy of God's plan. Violence was not completely averted. All four gospels say that one of Jesus' followers, who John identifies as Peter, drew a sword and cut the ear off a high priest's servant. Jesus immediately stepped in to prevent hostilities from escalating, but only Luke says he miraculously restored the ear. Then, Jesus challenged the guards, asking them why they felt they needed to bring weapons when they had all been around him in the Temple and on the streets and could have arrested him easily. With that, Matthew and Mark indicate that all but one of the disciples fled, a young man who Mark says was seized but escaped by literally running out of his garment, fleeing naked across the garden. There was no further resistance to Jesus' arrest.

Q *Jesus has asked you to watch with him as he prays. It's been a long day, and you can barely keep your eyes open. Can you watch with Jesus and pray with him? Whenever we begin to pray, we are called to focus our senses on the Lord in just such a way.*

Trials

The guards took Jesus and were accompanied by Judas as they returned to the dark side of the city and went in the Essene Gate. There they were met by retired high priest Annas, who led them to the home of Caiaphas. The Sanhedrin did not have a formal building at that time, and the palace of the high priest was the best place to secretly put Jesus on trial.

The reward for turning someone in at that time was thirty pieces of silver, which was so determined because it was equal to the price of a slave on the market. When Judas entered the reception hall of the palace, he was given a bag with thirty pieces of silver. Failure to accept it would have branded him a liar, and although there was no way they were going to release Jesus, Judas could have ended up sitting right next to him. At once the traitor realized what had happened. He was ignored when he tried to interrupt the proceedings, and eventually he was left out of them all together.

The longest day had begun. As modern Catholics celebrate the Triduum, it is designed to be a liturgy that continues for three days. It begins with the Lord's Supper on Holy Thursday and goes through the Easter Vigil on Saturday. In all, the celebration seems like one very long day, and the Mass for the Easter Vigil is the longest liturgy of the Church year, as it revisits the whole history of the faith. For Jesus, the few hours remaining of human life were agonizing testimony to great suffering and how much God was willing to give to bring his people home.

Jesus' immense suffering leading up to his death is well-known. It's a story of incredible violence and pure hatred, but beyond the passion there were other events unfolding. No story or character in the Holy Bible is without purpose. Caiaphas had a sometimes overlooked role in secular and Christian history. Barabbas was a caricature of evil against the goodness of Christ, and their story reveals much about the choices Christians make every day.

Joseph Caiaphas became high priest somewhere near the beginning of John the Baptist's ministry. By the time Jesus was arrested, Caiaphas was the third-most powerful man in Israel behind Pilate and Herod. He was quite open with his life of extravagance and opulence and never hesitated to wield his power.

When Jesus disrupted the market in the Temple and freed the holocaust offerings, Caiaphas was one of the biggest financial losers; like most of the other priests and elders, he had an investment in the profitable trade. Sometimes the biggest motivator for evil is not religion or politics, but pure and simple greed. Caiaphas was making a choice between the worldly and the heavenly. He meant to protect all that he had and not turn the other cheek as far as this Jesus was concerned.

The times were unstable. It was only five years earlier that Pontius Pilate's army brutally crushed what was deemed a peaceful protest at the Temple in Jerusalem. Less than three years after Jesus' execution, the procurator was recalled to Rome, replaced by Marcellus, who in turn replaced Caiaphas with Jonathan ben Ananus. The Bible is somewhat sympathetic to Pilate's position and what he was forced to do as a political pawn, while other limited and contradictory documents of the day suggest he was nothing more than a self-serving, brutal, and vicious conqueror. His true character was likely somewhere in between.

About thirty years later, the Romans finally moved beyond little skirmishes and launched a full-scale invasion of Jerusalem, which ended about three years later with the destruction of the Temple and much of the city. As for Pilate: He would barely be a footnote in history if it wasn't for his role in the death of Jesus; the New Testament keeps his name alive. Caiaphas and Pilate were indelibly linked forever. The high priest was appointed by the Roman governor and could just as easily have been removed by him.

The Temple was the most holy place for the expression of Jewish faith. At the time of Passover annually, multitudes of people went to Jerusalem and to the Temple. It was also the most fiscally appreciated time in all of Judea and perhaps the whole world.

There were trials and rituals required to enter the Temple area. First, one had to bathe in a pool called the miqvah at a price, then make a small sacrifice such as a dove at a reasonable price, and then pay an entry fee to the Temple. More charges were incurred once the man made it inside. It was profitable indeed, and Jesus brought it all down. When he spoke of destroying the Temple and rebuilding it in three days, many people of his time thought he was talking about the actual destruction of the building, which didn't happen until AD 70. The understanding from the Bible is that he was talking about his own Temple of life coming down in death and being resurrected in three days. However, he literally brought the Temple to a financial downfall that men like Caiaphas believed might last longer than three days.

The man who entered the Temple building had to be pure, and the more pure, the further in he could go. The marketplace that Jesus disrupted was on the Temple mound but was more like an outdoor, enclosed courtyard through which one passed to enter the building, and was large enough to house many animals and booths. It is unlikely that Jesus had the credentials to ever teach within the inner sanctum of the Temple, not that it would necessarily have stopped him, but it would have created a heightened state of alert among the Temple guards. However, many in the large crowd that had gathered at the Temple for Passover were there because of Jesus, whether friend, foe, or curious. There were too many people for him to teach on the inside anyway, so most of his addresses to them took place outside or in the courtyard, once he had cleared it. These are the people and places that witnessed the trials of Jesus Christ.

Q *Everyone experiences suffering in their lives, some greater than others. Many try to avoid it by political or monetary gains, as if they could delay any ordeal. Imagine the fear of materially oriented people like Pilate and Caiaphas when they thought Jesus might bring down their power. Do you hang onto possessions or position as a source of security?*

Who Is Barabbas?

Caiaphas was frightened. More Roman troops were in Jerusalem than had been at any time since he became high priest. To make matters worse, rumors surfaced that zealots known as Sicarii, "assassins" or "daggers," were hatching a plot to rebel that would likely kill many Romans and cause a tremendous reprisal. The high priest was a desperate man who moved to protect his position and wealth. He used the pretense of protecting the faith to circumvent the law and try Jesus on the trumped-up charge of blasphemy, turning it into a violation against Roman law: that the man had called himself a Messiah and king of the Jews. Jesus was therefore a threat to Roman *status quo*, a capital offense. It was easier for Caiaphas to convince Pilate than some may think.

By the time Caiaphas had convened the Sanhedrin, he had also decided Lazarus—known as Jesus' close friend—needed to go, too. Jesus' following was growing by the minute, partially because of what some believed was the raising of Lazarus from the dead.

Lazarus was a wealthy man, possibly a benefactor to the cause, but he appears by name only in John's Gospel. One school of thought is that Lazarus was the man who Jesus told to sell his possessions and give to the poor, but could not (mentioned in Matthew 19). Another study suggests that he was excluded from the synoptic gospels because he was still alive and in hiding, possibly concealed by the apostles themselves, when they were written. He was a disciple of Christ, as were his sisters, Martha and Mary, and was not arrested and crucified with the Lord.

Another major player in the events of Good Friday was a man whose name was Jesus bar Abbas, one who became known simply, throughout history as Barabbas. Jesus, or Yeshua, was a common name at the time. He was a leader of the treacherous assassins, Sicarii, and just the kind of person who would use the convenience of Passover and the centrally located presence of Roman soldiers to launch a bloody revolution. Mark, Luke, and John identify him as an insurrectionist or a revolutionary, with the first two evangelists calling him a murderer, as well. An insurrection did take place at an aqueduct near Jerusalem as pilgrims and soldiers filed into Jerusalem just days before Jesus' arrest, resulting in an ambush and the death of several Romans before the uprising was quelled.

Barabbas was well-known in Jerusalem as a hero because of his guerilla warfare against the oppressors. Several witnesses confirmed that he was at the aqueduct that day, and he killed Romans. He was too well-known to have been able to avoid capture or death for long, and the insurrection made it happen immediately. He was one of several men arrested following the uprising, although there is no indication he was ever charged with murder.

Historic texts, including Bible information, suppose that Pilate knew Caiaphas was a greedy and jealous man, and the case against Jesus was purely for those reasons. On the other hand, he understood that Barabbas was a savage murderer of Romans and fully expected to crucify him. Jesus could have saved himself by speaking up in his defense before Pilate, but that was not part of the prophecy. He was admired to some degree by Pilate, but instead of winning his support, the Lord's silence rendered the governor completely neutral, which fated the priests and elders to have their way. Pilate tried to pawn the decision off on his uneasily aligned opponent, King Herod Antipas, who was in Jerusalem at the time of Passover.

Luke's Gospel gives some details of Jesus' trip to Herod. The king was anxious to meet with him and hoped to see miracles but found the same stubborn response from the Galilean that Pilate did. It was Passover, and he was not in favor of executing Jews. Jesus was made fun of and pushed around, but the most humiliating thing Herod inflicted on him was to dress him in royal raiment and return him to Pilate, laughing and mocking his kingship, and declaring that he could not find a capital crime in him.

By the time Jesus was returned, Pilate's wife had informed him of a dream she had suffered because of Jesus. She warned her husband not to have anything to do with his execution. The governor informed the priests and elders that he found no guilt in the man and neither did Herod. The matter would have been done had the Sanhedrin not badgered Pilate into a false belief that the crucifixion of Jesus was the way to protect himself politically. Instead, Pilate would eventually end up being recalled to Rome to account for what happened that day, and he never returned to prominence.

A most curious set of circumstances took place after the governor tried to appease the Jews with a sufficient amount of torture on their captive, which didn't work. While Mark is the only gospel writer to specifically say there was a custom of releasing a prisoner for Passover, the other three allude to it. Historical records outside the Bible tell of no such custom existing in Judea. However, events of the same type did take place in other Roman provinces. A little coercion from the priests and Pilate apparently instituted the plan in Jerusalem, one time only.

The Antonia Fortress near the Temple grounds is where Pilate's troops were garrisoned and where Jesus was imprisoned by the soldiers who tortured him mercilessly. These were men of gladiator mentality, and viciousness was their code. Jesus and Barabbas were both brought to the old palace of King Herod the Great that faced a large open space, known as the Upper Market, which had filled up with people expecting some announcement. Since the high priests and elders had prompted this action, they had the advantage of being in the crowd along with their servants and soldiers. They made their presence known and used every means to secure a supportive crowd. They greased palms, they had people beaten and dragged away, and they stared down anyone who might act against them. Before Jesus and Barabbas even appeared on the balcony, the agents of the Sanhedrin had started a chant of "Crucify him!"

There is no indication that Barabbas was ever imprisoned in the same manner as Jesus. If he had killed a Roman soldier and was locked up with Roman soldiers, the tough revolutionary would likely have been beaten to death, while Jesus survived what should have been a fatal beating because he was the Christ. As is the case in any war or revolution, there are many sides to the same story, and it is probable Barabbas had a connection within a Roman faction. Everything pointed to Jesus being the one who would die.

Pilate himself may have actually believed the crowd would pick Jesus over Barabbas for release. That was certainly what he intended to happen. Three times he berated Barabbas, calling him every name and repeating the crimes he was charged with. The intimidation of the crowd by the priests and elders was one thing, but they were also persuaded by the fact Barabbas was a hero. By shouting out his crimes, Pilate only reaffirmed that the prisoner was a revolutionary against the Roman oppressors, which was regaled by the Jews. The courtyard got louder each time the calls for Barabbas' release and Jesus' crucifixion rang out.

Q *Barabbas and Jesus were opposites, and the choice made between them reflects aggression, hostility, hate, and anger versus peace, compassion, love, and service to others. Barabbas may have been a religious man, but his methods were not of God's plan. We make a choice to be like Barabbas or Jesus every day. Who do you choose most often? What intimidations and bribes sway choices today from heavenly to the worldly?*

The Sentence

Reluctantly, Pilate gave in, but the governor was not without a plan for retribution. He had three scaffolds set up for crucifixion that day. Then Pilate determined who, after Barabbas, were the next worst revolutionaries he had captured. Two men hanged on each side of Jesus as revenge for Roman lives that were taken.

For most of the Christian era those two men have been called robbers. In the *New American Bible*, Matthew and Mark call them revolutionaries, and Luke calls them criminals. The Greek word for robber easily translates into the other words, as well, and Rome did not crucify thieves. The two men were likely looters and pillagers, zealots who took part in killing Roman soldiers at the aqueduct. Without trial, they replaced their leader, who was the only one Pilate had expected to die that day. There is no confirmed record of what happened to Barabbas after his release. There were many insurrections over the next few years, and he may well have died in one of them or eventually been executed.

Caiaphas, Pilate, Barabbas, and even Lazarus represented different faith personalities in the parable of Jesus' arrest, trial, and subsequent execution. Caiaphas was given a choice of what was more important to him: his position and wealth or spiritual honesty and integrity. An image of him might be: As everyone else runs away from a disaster, he is going back, trying to gather his belongings to take with him. Like many others, Lazarus was simply afraid of dying. He chose Christ but hid rather than trusting in the Lord's deliverance. So did the other disciples. Pilate knew what the right choice was but allowed himself to be intimidated into choosing the opposite, compounded by his exacting revenge, letting someone else suffer for his erroneous decision.

Barabbas was the symbol of evil, craved by the people more than the goodness of Christ. With bribery or intimidation the crowd was led to choose evil over good. Many were the same people who greeted Jesus on Palm Sunday or heard him at the Temple. Some that turned against him were even longtime followers. Some, who were steadfast in their faith, just didn't speak up loud enough. It was as if they didn't know any better, but surely they did. We are asked everyday, "Do you choose Barabbas or do you choose Christ?

And Jesus? Throughout his last days he became the perfect example of prayer and communion. He humbly carried on God's plan, even though he had doubts. He became open to the Father's presence in his life and listened to the voice of a Holy Spirit. He loved the Father and cared for his people. He was one with God. He was one with us, our sacrifice and our Savior. He was sentenced to die, that his gift would never be forgotten.

Q *Sometimes when we make the wrong choice, others suffer for our mistake. Walk with Christ and think of how much he gave by being wrongly accused and condemned. Make a commitment to think more like Jesus in the choices you make.*

On the Cross

There always have been and always will be random opinions and questions about the crucifixion of Jesus Christ: Where was it, how was the cross constructed, and where was his tomb? In the early fourth century, Saint Helena discovered what was believed to be the three crosses, including the one of the Savior. Among the churches she had built was the one on Calvary at the crucifixion site. In modern times, layers of archeological discoveries have challenged the exact location, but Church historians of the latter fourth century attested to Saint Helena's findings.

Once Jesus' royal raiment was removed and he was again in his own clothes and led out into the street, a crowd formed that grew and followed him to the place of his execution, Golgotha, "the place of the skull." It was the Roman way that he would have only been carrying the crossbar that would affix to a "tree," a wooden scaffold that formed the upright support of the cross. It was not that common for a criminal to carry his own cross alone. The wood was too heavy for one man to carry up the hill or out on the road into town. Jesus may have started the journey bearing his cross alone. Even so, the wood grew heavier because of his deteriorating condition. He may not have made it to the crucifixion site had the soldiers not enlisted the aid of a man named Simon.

Mark casually mentions Simon as the father of Alexander and Rufus without further clarification, which suggests that the evangelist's audience would have known who they were. He came "in from the country," which further suggests that, although Simon came from Cyrene, he was probably living or temporarily staying somewhere in Judea. He may have been in Jerusalem because of Passover. John is the only gospel writer who doesn't name Simon as someone who helped carry the crossbeam, but rather he says, Jesus carried the cross to Golgotha himself. No Roman soldiers helped Jesus in any way, even though they feared punishment if he died before they got to Calvary. The simple truth is that the soldiers were being delayed by the weakened Jesus, and there was absolutely no chance any of them would lower themselves to help carry the cross, so they grabbed the strongest man in sight and forced his enlistment.

In his letter to the Romans, Paul identifies a Christian, Rufus, as someone he knew for a long time, possibly in Jerusalem. Scholars have theorized that because of this mention, it is likely Simon's family—if not already followers of Jesus—converted to his teaching after the crucifixion.

Only Luke tells of the women of Jerusalem during the Way of the Cross, who walked with Jesus, close enough to carry on a conversation with him. They walked all the way to the place of the crucifixion, and at least some stayed. The gospel writers identify a variety of women at the cross, never directly linking them to the group who walked along the way with the Lord. All of the evangelists name Jesus' mother Mary, and also Mary, the mother of James and John, and Mary Magdalene as those who kept the vigil with Jesus. Luke adds Joanna to the list, and Mark says Salome was there. All of these women were known to be disciples of Jesus.

Also, on the cross there was apparently a sign identifying the victim. All four gospel writers agree that the inscription identified him as "King of the Jews." However, John tells a story of bickering behind the scenes. It was a holy season for the Jews, and the inscription was written in all languages accommodating the pilgrims in and around Jerusalem. The high priests went to Pilate and told him the inscription should read that he claimed to be king of the Jews, not that he was. The procurator, probably still angered that Barabbas wasn't hanging there, announced there would be no change in the insulting sign.

When Jesus was crucified, he was offered a wine concoction not mentioned by John and referred to only as wine by Luke. Matthew and Mark both say it included a drug identified as myrrh. They both say he refused it, although Matthew notes that Jesus did taste it first. No doubt the drug was meant as a painkiller, but as with any other drug of the kind, taken in a large amount could be fatal. Jesus had three choices: no myrrh, enough myrrh to kill the pain, or enough to die. Once he knew what the wine contained, he declined to take it, thus guaranteeing he would feel every shred of pain the nails in his hands, the beating across his back, and the thorns piercing his forehead would create. Jesus chose to die in pain, fulfilling the will of the Father and the prophecies that had been foretold.

Of those prophecies, some were contained in the psalms. As Jesus' possessions—literally the clothes on his back—were being divided and auctioned off, he recited from Psalm 22, the prophecy declaring just such a thing would happen. Most of the time Jesus was conscious on the cross, he was praying and what he was praying was Scripture.

In the last hours as Jesus hung on the cross, the synoptic gospels of Matthew, Mark, and Luke all talk about darkness hanging over the whole area from noon until three, very possibly the length of time Jesus was alive during the crucifixion. Luke says the darkness was caused by an eclipse, but three hours is a long solar eclipse on anybody's schedule. When the darkness ended, all manner of things began to happen. The great curtain in the Temple was torn from top to bottom, and earthquakes shook to the point of graves opening up. Ghosts appeared as if living flesh everywhere. It is no wonder that everyone was frightened. Jesus prayed out loud with his last gasp of breath and gave it over to the Father, as he said, "It is finished."

Q *Modern Christians venerate the cross on Good Friday. Many make pilgrimages to holy sites both in the Middle East and within their own communities throughout the world. This is a time to contemplate how our sins caused such great suffering in someone who was so good.*

The Burial of Jesus

Matthew, Mark, and Luke all agree that the women who had followed Jesus from Galilee were there to the very end, but John adds an exchange that took place among himself, the Savior, and Mary, Mother of the Lord. Jesus told them to look at each other as mother and son, and in this way confirm their care of each other as family. This was when Christ delivered all people into each other's hands and into the arms of his Mother. John immediately took her into his care, and eventually to his home in Ephesus, where Mary's house was built and still stands.

Once Jesus died, others began to show up. Roman centurions were the first, given the unpleasant task of breaking the legs of any victims still alive as they made their rounds. The purpose of this was so the legs could no longer support the weight of the body, which would then collapse in on the lungs and bring about suffocation faster. When they saw that Jesus was already dead, they chose not to break his legs, but instead pierced his side with a lance. Jesus did not expel bodily fluids prior to death, but poured forth blood and water from the new wound immediately after it was inflicted. It was miraculous that he was living even in death. When all of these things passed, as witnessed by John, people were heard to say, "Truly, this was the Son of God."

Joseph of Arimathea was a secret follower of Jesus' and an influential, ranking member of the Sanhedrin. Although all four gospels acknowledge his role, none of them ever explain why or by who he was summoned to take charge after the crucifixion. Joseph was a wealthy merchant from a place called Arimathea (Ramathaim) in the northern area of Judea, but his fortune was made in Jerusalem. Because of his fiscal stature and authority, he was able to approach Pilate without delay. Using one of those old Jewish customs that Pilate never seemed to understand, he asked for quick removal of the body and that it be turned over to him for burial before the beginning of the Sabbath, just a few hours away. It was a normal practice of Romans to leave bodies on the crosses for the vultures and other scavengers, but this was Passover season, and it was not unusual for the priests to request crucified victims be moved out of sight of the transportation routes.

The Jerusalem elite could afford tombs that were significant family sites, but Jesus was not considered of a social class deserving of such a tomb. Greek-architectured family tombs of Jesus' time may still be seen today in Jerusalem, such as the tomb of Zacharias. Some of the burial customs predated the ancient Hebrews' arrival in Canaan. In that tradition, Joseph of Arimathea had the Lord taken to his family tomb. Under any other circumstances, Jesus would not have had such a lavish grave hewn from rock.

Some of the women who stayed with Jesus, led by Mary Magdalene, went with Joseph so they would know where the tomb was. Time had run out. The Sabbath was about to begin, and they would have to wait until its conclusion before they could prepare to anoint the body and hold the funeral of the Lord.

Also involved was Nicodemus, who was a secret follower of Jesus' and a Sanhedrin member almost from the beginning of John's Gospel. His stature was similar to that of Joseph, and he paid for all or part of the expenses of Jesus' burial and anointing.

It would have been a disaster for Joseph or Nicodemus to be found out by the Sanhedrin. Their actions would have destroyed their reputation and any credibility they had with the organization. Matthew infers that some of the priests did find out that Jesus was removed from the cross, and they went in committee to Pilate. They told him there was likely a conspiracy under way in which the apostles might very well steal the body and claim him to be risen as he prophesied. They petitioned the Roman to have the tomb sealed, at least for three days, with a guard on it. He agreed, and despite one long-held belief, there were no Roman guards overnight at the tomb, and none of the gospels ever says there were. Matthew says the procurator told the Jews to use their own guards to seal and protect the site, and that they did.

In a quarry at the Church of the Holy Sepulcher, archeologists have identified the tombs of Nicodemus and Joseph, thus proving the burial place of the Christ is where Saint Helena discovered it to be. The Lord was placed on a shelf in this joint family tomb, as described in the gospels. It was customary to have a "rolling rock" that could readily be rolled into place. Since it was possible to roll the stone back and forth, no one knows if Jesus' friends closed it or if the Pharisee guards sealed the tomb later.

As for the tomb being opened, only Matthew tells a fantastic story of a great earthquake, followed by the descent from heaven of an angel who rolled back the stone and took a seat on it. God's messenger relayed the Lord's instructions to the women, that they go tell the disciples and for all of them to go to Galilee, where they would see Jesus. The other three gospels do not address how the stone was moved, only that Jesus was no longer in the tomb.

Q *Imagine the sense of loss that seized the followers of Jesus when they heard he was dead. All sorts of things must have passed through their minds, and they fled or hid from the fear that they might be next. Have you ever perceived that God's love would not protect you? Consider those times when you were sure that it would.*

Part II: The First Days With Jesus

Who Is Mary Magdalene?

What if Mary Magdalene was a writer, a teacher of faith, and the apostle to the apostles? What if she was Jesus' main confidante? What if she provided the financing of his mission? Her role may never be completely known. In the meantime, her name will continue to be linked to controversy and legend. Although there isn't a lot written about Miriam of Magdala in the Holy Bible, she is mentioned more than any other female in the New Testament. She is at the forefront of men and women disciples.

At different times in Church history, she has been called a prostitute, the sister of Martha and Lazarus, and the wife of Jesus (*The Da Vinci Code* was not the first time that was suggested.) None of these claims have any substantiated evidence to back them up. Artists have portrayed her as a lusty woman, sometimes with flaming red hair, and others have drawn her as solemnly as they did the Virgin Mother. Poetry, fact, and fictional stories about her have been around for centuries.

Who is Mary Magdalene?

The mystery woman was a victim of gender bias after Jesus' ascension, perhaps even before, and the prostitute story apparently came from a mistake. In the last verses of the seventh chapter of Luke's Gospel, the evangelist tells the story of a very sinful woman who literally throws herself on Jesus' feet when he was a guest in a Pharisee's house. She washed them with her tears and dried them with her hair. Jesus forgave her sins, and despite the Pharisee's protest, he told the woman to go in peace, as her faith had saved her. Chapter eight begins immediately talking about Jesus' ministry, traveling from town to town. He was accompanied by others, including the twelve apostles and women who had been cured or freed of their demons, and they were Joanna, Susanna, and Mary Magdalene. Some associated Mary Magdalene with the prostitute in the previous story. Since that woman wasn't given a name, she could just as easily have been Joanna or Susanna, or anyone. This myth was compounded when Pope Gregory I made the same gospel comparison during a homily in 591, and she was branded. Most modern scholars agree that there is nothing to back up such a claim. Incidentally, the unnamed woman in chapter seven was never called a prostitute in the gospel, nor are her sins defined. Mark and Luke remind that Mary Magdalene is in fact the woman who had seven demons driven from her by Jesus. Neither tells where, when, or how.

The woman from Magdala was probably just the opposite of the caricature of her. Since she was never called Mary of Bethany, there is no reason to believe she had any relationship with Lazarus and his two sisters. If she associated with the likes of Joanna and Susanna, she almost certainly had money. Further on in the eighth chapter of Luke's Gospel, he says those women provided financial support for Jesus' ministry out of their own resources. Luke also reveals these women, who had followed him from Galilee, were at the crucifixion, and he names Joanna with Mary Magdalene at the tomb.

Luke is the only gospel that talks about Mary Magdalene before the passion of our Lord, and when she appears in Matthew, Mark, and John, the saint is treated like a person the reader should already be acquainted with, which—some scholars insist—proves she was once well-known among the disciples. Some believe she was the sister of the apostle Philip.

The best-known story of Mary Magdalene from the New Testament is her discovery of Jesus' resurrection. In all four gospels, she and companions are met by angels who send them to inform the disciples. In Mark and John she is identified as the first person to see the risen Lord. Matthew says the women first saw him when they were on their way to tell the disciples of the angel's message. In Mark's story, the women fled from the tomb and did not immediately go to tell the disciples, but Mary Magdalene stayed at the tomb until daybreak and then went to the apostles. To one degree or another, the gospels insinuate that the apostles, especially Peter, did not believe the story. In three of the gospels, he does lead John and others to check the story out, but it is left inconclusive, mentioning only Peter's amazement. In John's telling of the story, the beloved disciple and Peter returned to the apostles while Mary stayed behind. It was then that she met the risen Lord face to face. Mary Magdalene left their meeting and went to the apostles to tell what she had seen. They apparently did not believe her.

In 1896, a document was discovered that became part of the Nag Hammadi Library. The work was originally written in the Coptic (Egyptian) language. It first appeared in English in 1977. In declaring the canon, the Church fathers disallowed the Gospel of Mary Magdalene, a relatively unknown document even then, although rumors of its existence persisted through the centuries. In it, Mary describes the scene when she reveals special secret teachings that were given only to her by Jesus. Andrew refused to believe, saying Jesus would never have spoken that way, and Peter chastised her, challenging that Jesus would never trust a woman with his message. Fortunately, the gospels somewhat support that the disciples refused to believe her, but they also suggest Jesus' attitude toward women was different from the apostles and the custom they grew up with. His conversations with women like the Samaritan woman at the well, in talking to the women as he carried the cross, and most especially to Mary Magdalene would indicate Jesus' feelings toward them. He chose her to announce his resurrection.

In modern times, Mary Magdalene serves as a unique example of Christian life. In symbol or reality, she may have committed all seven deadly sins but somehow rose above them to reform her life and follow Jesus to the ends of the earth. Like everyone else, she sinned but managed to find Christ and overcome her sadness, becoming part of his salvation given to all. The Church has instructed that she should be remembered for those things known at the cross and tomb and not by the erroneous personalities of other women in the gospels. Mary Magdalene was the first witness to the death, burial, and the resurrection of the Lord.

Q *Mary Magdalene displayed immense love for our Lord and in so doing serves as an example for us all. How do you demonstrate deep love for Jesus? Do you recover from your sins by forgiving yourself and asking God to forgive you, too? Consider that his response is unconditional love for you.*

Easter Sunday: As Morning Breaks

One date suggested for the resurrection of the Lord is April 9, AD 30, not really a scientific discovery, but it serves to remind us that Jesus rose from the dead in the springtime. It was sometime before sunrise, and a slim moonlit sky lay over Jerusalem. In the cemetery, each tomb had its own spot, a garden where blooms were beginning to open along with trees with buds that would soon yield fruit, a special place for those laid to rest and the living who pray and meditate with them.

Emerging from the dark path, Mary Magdalene led a group of women. They planned to pray with the Lord as they anointed him and prepared him for the proper burial that had been delayed for the entire Sabbath and most of the night that followed.

At the burial place for the family of Joseph of Arimathea, they stopped in the garden and prayed for God's guidance in what they were about to do. The women had heard that a stone had been wheeled into place, and one of their prayer requests was that someone would help them roll back the blockade. As they approached the tomb entrance, no Pharisee guards were found, but their help wasn't needed, as the stone had already been rolled away from the entrance.

The sounds of spring filled the air even though there was an eeriness to it. The chirping birds and whistling breeze were reminders of new life about to begin. The other women stayed back as Mary Magdalene approached the tomb. It was haloed by a sliver of rising sun on the horizon. Even though she was somewhat frightened, it was as if a shout of joy was welling up inside her. When she looked inside, she saw the shelf where Jesus' body no longer laid. The space was covered only by his wrappings, but nearby stood a being in white seemingly giving off light. He told her that he knew she was seeking Jesus and announced to Mary Magdalene that the Lord had risen. He instructed her to go to Peter and the disciples to tell them what she had seen and that they should go at once to Galilee, where they would see him.

While the other women lost their way and hid together in the garden, Mary Magdalene ran off to where Peter and the apostles were hiding. She gave them the angel's instructions, but they did not completely believe. Mary reasoned that the body wasn't in the tomb, and they had no choice but to believe the instructions were real. Peter grabbed the boy apostle, John, since he was athletic and available, and hurried to the tomb. John, being the sprinter, got there well ahead of the heavy-set old fisherman, but, being young, did not go in. Mary and Peter arrived simultaneously, but only Peter went beyond the entrance of the tomb. What he found was exactly as Mary Magdalene described. The linens and napkin for his head that had been wrapped around the Lord were piled on the shelf. First, this was proof that no one had taken him away, because they would have had to explain why they were carrying a naked, dead body through the streets of Jerusalem. Second, although Peter was reluctant to admit it, Mary Magdalene might have been telling the truth...he is risen. In his Gospel, John says he went into the tomb after Peter and witnessed the same sight.

Peter huffed off with John in tow. He just walked away from Mary Magdalene and navigated to where the apostles were hiding. Peter immediately called everyone to order so he could reveal his findings and discern their next move. If it was Jesus calling them, everything would be safe, but if it was a trick, they would surely die on the open road to Galilee.

Mary Magdalene wept as she prayed in the garden. It was hard to know what was true. She wanted to believe that Jesus had risen, but she, too, was afraid that the whole thing could be a conspiracy to assemble his followers for capture.

"Why are you weeping?" the calm voice asked her.

She looked at the man who was silhouetted by the rising sun with a great aura, and in the shadow, she could not see his face. She thought he must be the caretaker for the burial site and she confessed, "My Lord is gone, and I don't know where they have taken him."

The stranger pressed on, "Woman, why are you weeping; who are you looking for?"

Mary was beside herself, racked with tears and remorse as she replied, "Please, if you have moved my Master, tell me where. I will take him." Weeping overtook her and she was near collapse.

"Miriam!" was all he said in his soft, yet strong, distinctive voice.

It was like being lifted out of her body and right into the arms of God. The weeping stopped instantly, and the joy exploded inside of her. She knew immediately who called her by name, and she responded in Hebrew, "*Rabbouni!*"

Q *Mary Magdalene ran the full gamut of emotions that first Easter morning. Embrace your feelings of sorrow at the Lord's suffering and death, and also the joy of his resurrection. Do you feel powerful emotions in loving God through Jesus Christ?*

The Aftermath

Jesus told Mary Magdalene that there were too many, her included, who were holding on to him. They must rise as he showed them and be gracious witnesses of the good news. He wanted her to become the teacher and to tell his disciples that his prophecy would be fulfilled in them. She needed to show the disciples that as Jesus is of the Father, so the Father is of him, and for all of them, too. If they didn't go forth and tell the gospel, then the truth would just as likely die on that hillside. Mary prayed with the Lord, and when he left her, she returned to the apostles.

In the meantime, the women who had gone to the tomb with Mary Magdalene had gathered their senses and moved from the garden onto the road that would take them to where the disciples were hidden. As they were on their way, they encountered Jesus in the early-morning light. These women were able to recognize him and touched his wounded feet for proof. Then they worshiped him, though once afraid of his disappearance from the tomb, they all became staunch believers in Jesus the Lord. He reassured them and they rushed off to finish their mission by telling the apostles, who were still not ready to believe he had risen.

The Sanhedrin quickly summoned the Pharisee soldiers assigned to guard the tomb for an accounting of what took place in the graveyard that night. Depending on who's telling the story, the guards either slept through it all, got frightened and ran away, or witnessed a miracle that they weren't prepared to talk about. Deciding that their variety of stories would never get them past any inquisitors, the priests paid them and instructed them to the man: What happened was that followers of Jesus came to the tomb while the guards slept. The men were awakened to the sight of Jesus' body being carried away by his disciples, but the soldiers were unable to prevent their escape.

The news was withheld from Pontius Pilate for as long as possible. Jesus appeared to several people at different times and places during the day of his resurrection. Other than those already mentioned, the two most significant sightings happened, first, to two disciples fleeing Jerusalem, then to the apostles themselves in their hiding place.

Q *Psalm 62:9 says, "Trust God at all times, my people! Pour out your hearts to God our refuge!" In the hours of Easter morning, people for and against Jesus were scrambling to discover the truth or perhaps hide it. The apostles saw things they didn't believe while others believed things they didn't see. Faith is trusting God. Say this affirmation daily: "I trust in God at all times."*

Emmaus: A Road to Life

The details of an incident that happened on the road from Jerusalem to Emmaus on that first Easter Sunday appear only in the Gospel of Luke, but they serve as a blueprint to the liturgical life of the Church even today. The event is best examined in four parts, the same four parts that comprise the celebration of the Eucharistic Liturgy.

The Passover festivities were ending, but Jerusalem was still a crowded place. As they had done since Jesus' arrest, the apostles were hiding. Some of his followers meant to leave Jerusalem altogether before a witch hunt could begin.

Two such disciples, one known as Cleopas and one who is unnamed, were scurrying away in the direction of their hometown, Emmaus. As they traveled they talked incessantly about what had happened over the last few days. The journey was going well, when a stranger joined their walk. He was the resurrected Jesus, but they did not recognize him.

Modern Sunday-morning churchgoers arrive as travelers on a certain road. They, too, are disappointed and discouraged. When Jesus asked the men what they were talking about, Cleopas mocked him, asking if he was the only person who didn't know what happened in Jerusalem. Jesus asked for an explanation, and they shared all their misgivings.

Those in church today also ask questions, trying to identify, understand, and forge a Christian identity. Liturgy begins when the congregation tells their story, as did the two disciples. They told Jesus: They believed in the Messiah who had been arrested and put to death on the cross. They proclaimed the Nazarene was truly a mighty prophet and they believed he was the answer to every problem in the world. He spoke for God to all people. They hoped he would be the one to lift up Israel. But their story got worse as they went along. The two told Jesus that the body laid in the tomb was gone when the women arrived to anoint him. Those same women went back to the apostles and said they had seen a vision of an angel who told them, "The Lord is risen."

"We did not believe and have faith," the pair told Jesus, "So some of us who followed him went to see for ourselves, and the tomb was just as the women said. Now what are we to do?"

The Liturgy of the Word, which is a proclamation of Scripture and the guiding hand of a homily (sermon) was first revealed as Jesus responded to the comments of his demoralized traveling companions. He told them they were foolish and slow of heart to not look more deeply into the words of the prophets. What happened in Jerusalem had long been foretold from Moses, down through the ages. Jesus spoke knowledgeably of things that had been and things yet to come.

He assured them that the final chapter had not been written. The two disciples found a new joy and new spirit.

The first half of the journey was over, and new life was being revealed. The disciples were so anxious to continue the life lesson that they pleaded with Jesus to stay overnight, to eat, rest, and by all means, teach. His destination would wait another day. The Eucharistic Liturgy is also at a midway point following the Scripture readings. The two disciples had told their story and then listened to Jesus tell THE story. The congregation in church has told their story and listened to God's. Much like the two disciples, the assembly in church is thirsty for more. The community should be pleading with Jesus to sit, to eat, help rest their busy lives, and just be with them. That's what he did then and what he does now.

Q *Sometimes we react to something before we have all the facts. When reading the Bible, one should take small portions and stop to meditate on them. The gospels truly speak the words of Jesus for our understanding. Going forward, make a resolution to open all your senses during the Liturgy of the Word at Mass and allow God's words to reach you.*

Our Hearts Were Burning

Having been first relieved and reconciled before being educated, the two disciples on the road to Emmaus were then ready for the big burst of energy that Jesus wanted to give them. Participants in the liturgy today also have experienced relief and reconciliation and were educated by the word of God. Just like travelers walking with Jesus, the faithful invite him into their lives and prepare for one big burst of spiritual energy.

There is no more fitting response to our need than the Communion with each other that Jesus lays on the table before us. Just like the glorious sacrament he instituted at the Last Supper, he brings the blessing of God, which we offer back to him with prayerful intent. The Eucharist is alive within each person that receives it, and it even touches lives of those who, for one reason or another, are unable to share the physical part of the meal.

The spirit of the risen Lord is before us. So too, this sacramental presence overcame the two disciples at Emmaus. Once Jesus had agreed to come into their home and hearts, once they had made welcome this stranger they were ready for the fire that burns inside. They placed bread, wine, and other food on the table before their welcome guest. Jesus took charge for that moment in their lives. He offered the bread to God, asked for the Father's blessing, and broke it. It was like a lightning bolt had just hit the room. The two disciples looked at each other, then at Jesus, then at each other again, both proclaiming simultaneously, "It's him! It's the Master." By the time they had gotten the words out of their mouths, their faces were lit up with utmost hope and anticipation, but when they turned back to Jesus, he was no longer there.

The two disciples had recognized Jesus suddenly, and they responded with one of the finest statements ever made, "Were not our hearts burning within us as he spoke to us and opened the Scripture to us?" Modern Christians have experienced that burning sensation, too, the hearing of God's word and the fire which Jesus gave to us not only by his words but also his actions. The cup we drink is a communion in Christ's blood, and the bread we eat is our share in his body. Like the two disciples, the church community doesn't recognize the face of Jesus among their group either, but they know his presence is with them like a fire in the heart and soul. To commune with Jesus is why the two disciples, the apostles, and all Christians after them do this…and remember.

When the two at Emmaus had gathered their wits about them, they went forth in a very big way to love and serve the Lord and to share the good news of his resurrection. Luke's Gospel reveals that the two departed immediately and apparently returned to Jerusalem even faster than they left it. They found the apostles and other disciples in hiding and told them the whole story of what had happened on the road to Emmaus and how Jesus became known to them in the breaking of the bread. Luke goes on to say that while they were still speaking, Jesus stood among them, and his first words were, "Peace be with you."

Mark is the only other evangelist who refers to the Emmaus journey, and it is barely a footnote, without any details of the encounter. He mentions that this incident was the next time after Mary Magdalene that Jesus appeared to anyone and that the two disciples ran back to tell the apostles, who did not believe them.

After the journey to Emmaus and throughout the universal Church community today, there is still the fourth part which brings it all together. At worship, the faithful have brought their story before the Lord and each other. They have listened as the Scripture was broken open for their deeper commitment and understanding. A bond is shared with each other and our Savior, by tasting the sacrifice he made for us, and inviting him into our hearts. The celebration is not over. After the final prayer of the Communion Rite, the assembly is given God's blessing and dismissed with the words, "Our Mass is ended. Go forth to love and serve the Lord" (More and more priests are adding "and each other" to the end of that expression, and rightly so).

Q *Are not our hearts burning within us? Picture Mass' four parts as described on the road to Emmaus. Consider the Penitential Rite when we tell our story and ask for forgiveness. Relax and listen to the words of the Old and New Testament, the wisdom that is given to those who listen. Let Jesus in your heart and see his presence during Communion. Go forth and share these things with others that they might know. Do you feel differently about the Eucharistic Liturgy after hearing how it came about on the road to Emmaus?*

Second Sunday of Easter

In Luke's words, at least one of the apostles told the two disciples from Emmaus that Peter saw the Lord, perhaps overly enthusiastic, because none of the four gospels tell of a meeting between Peter and Jesus until after he had appeared before all of the apostles. However, the meeting he had with all of them was an incredible spiritual experience.

Although all four evangelists write that Jesus appeared to all the disciples later in the day on that first Easter Sunday, only John tells the popular story of "Doubting Thomas," which is the gospel read in church on the Second Sunday of Easter every year. According to him, the story actually spans two Sundays. The gospels call the day of Jesus' resurrection, "the first day of the week." That, having been a Sunday, became known in Christian faith as the Lord's Day, a memorial to his resurrection that has been remembered every Sunday since, distinguishing itself from the traditional Sabbath of the Jewish people, although the connection between the two should not be forgotten.

There is a non-canonical gospel known as the Gospel of Nicodemus, which some scholars believe is a contrived recounting of the events around the Lord's death, which was actually produced by Christians some time later, perhaps the third century. According to "Nicodemus," when word finally got to Pilate that the stone had been rolled back and the tomb was empty, he suspected every possibility and every person. He closed the gates of the city and went to the Sanhedrin, demanding to know if they had a great book of prophecy. When that was confirmed, he insisted on being told, with the threat of death for lying, whether or not there was prophecy about Jesus Christ anywhere in it. The high priests Caiaphas and his father-in-law, Annas, confessed that they thought Jesus used trickery to perform miracles, and they didn't believe he was the one prophesied in those books. Already there were witnesses who claimed to have seen Jesus alive after his death.

The disciples were at table, hidden away with locks on doors and windows. Because they were frightened and in fear for their lives, a guard was posted outside, and further, the sentry could've been Thomas on that particular hour. Jesus didn't come up the path, but ethereally appeared in the room with them; anyone outside wouldn't have seen him.

The two disciples from Emmaus were still telling their story, Luke says, when the Lord appeared in the hiding place known as the upper room (but not the same upper room that was used for the Passover feast). That location was well-known and too close to the activity of the city. Jesus said, "Peace be with you," but they were still frightened by him. Even then, he showed them his hands and feet bearing the wounds of the crucifixion, and they continued to be afraid. In Luke's version, Jesus ate baked fish in front of them to prove he wasn't a ghost.

In Mark's telling of the story, Jesus rebuked them for their hardness of heart and because they didn't believe those who had claimed to see him risen from the dead. Luke adds that Jesus sat down with them and taught the meaning of the Scriptures, and their minds were opened by him to understanding the word. He told the disciples that with the prophecy fulfilled, "repentance for the forgiveness of sins" was to be preached in his name to all nations. He said this was the day that marked the first witnesses of "these things" emerging from Jerusalem.

In Mark, Jesus tells how to accomplish these things. He tells his followers to go out into the world to teach and exemplify the "good news" they had witnessed. He said baptism and belief in the gospel were the roads to salvation, and that those who believe in him would be able to do many great things by the will of the Father.

Not only did John reveal that Jesus sent them out, but that he gave them authority to preside over the sacraments, specifically baptism and reconciliation. He breathed on them and told them to receive the Holy Spirit. Jesus was talking about an event yet to happen, and so, according to Luke, he warned them to remain where they were in Jerusalem until they had received the Spirit. Jesus left them the same way he appeared, and it was all done in the absence of Thomas.

Q *Many believe the seven sacraments set the Catholic Church apart from other Christian faiths. Baptism and Christian burial are universal to Christian churches, but in between there are differences. The sacraments of reconciliation and Eucharist are the primary ones we may receive over and over. How frequently do you take advantage of these two grace-filled sacraments?*

The Real Saint Thomas

Certainly all of the apostles had their intimate moments with the Lord, and some of them proved great teaching experiences, but very few of them appear in the Bible. The synoptic gospels list twelve apostles but discuss relatively nothing of their experiences as individuals. For private counsel and special teaching, Jesus always took Peter, James, and John with him, and sometimes Andrew was included. One apostle's story that does appear is the popular "Doubting Thomas." However, the standard interpretation of who Thomas was based on is a misrepresentation of all that he did in the years of Jesus' earthly ministry and for a long time thereafter.

In John's Gospel, the personality of Thomas, called Didymus, is first introduced in chapter eleven as Jesus prepared for the journey to Bethany and the grave of Lazarus. According to John, the wheels of injustice were already in motion. Jesus and his followers knew he was a marked man and could be arrested at any time. Bethany was close to Jerusalem and was a place that would be filled with mourners for the popular Lazarus and with followers of Jesus. It was too dangerous a place for Jesus to walk unescorted, a fact that was noted by Thomas, who insisted the apostles all go along. Perhaps they would try to protect him, but, as Thomas said, they would die with Jesus if that was God's will. His loyalty and bravery were clear. In response, the apostles did go with him and thereby became even greater witnesses to the Lord.

On Easter Sunday, John reveals that when Thomas finally arrived, the apostles were clamoring to tell him what happened. They almost certainly told him about the wounds on Jesus' body. Thomas gave the response one would expect from a man of his ilk. He told them he didn't believe it, and if he was ever going to, he would also have to see Jesus' hands and feet and touch the wound in his side. Thomas was only asking for what the others had already received without asking. The gospel says a week later Jesus did return, and he again offered, "Peace be with you," before directly addressing Thomas. He instructed him to touch and examine the wounds. The apostle followed Jesus' instructions and proclaimed him Lord and God. Jesus did not put him down but reminded the apostle that he only believed after he saw proof, but there are those who haven't seen and yet believe.

What of those apostles who were not called doubters, but who were hidden away, not only on Easter Sunday, but a week later, after they had already witnessed the Lord and were professed to believe? For them and especially for Thomas, the ministry had only just begun.

After that, Thomas is mentioned one more time by John. Seven of the disciples had gathered at Lake Tiberius, one of many names for the Sea of Galilee. They went fishing with Peter and stayed out all night, catching nothing. At dawn they saw Jesus on the shore but did not recognize him, although they did submit to his request that they throw the nets off the right side of the boat. They caught so many fish that they weren't able to pull in the nets and had to drag them ashore. In the midst of this, John asserted that it was the Lord standing on the beach. In his telling of the story, the apostles ate breakfast cooked over a fire that Jesus built. As he ate, Jesus was finally recognized by all of them.

Q *A definition of faith is complete trust and confidence in someone or something. For all who believe in God, it is trusting and having confidence in something in evidence all around us, yet not readily accessible to our earthly senses. Think of the things you believe are proof of God in our lives. Are they enough to dispel your doubts?*

Jesus Appears in Galilee

The synoptic gospels all report one appearance with the apostles, and other disciples sometime soon after the resurrection of the Lord. However, they may not all be writing about the same appearance. John tells of that first appearance, and a second in the presence of Thomas, and even a third, when Jesus sent the seven out on Lake Tiberius. With the exception of that appearance, all others were presumed to take place in Jerusalem...all but one.

When Matthew describes the first meeting with Jesus, eleven apostles were in Galilee, as they had been instructed through Mary Magdalene. There is no mention that she or any other disciples went along. Matthew wrote for a strict Jewish audience that needed to be reassured that Jesus was one of them, a valid reason why Mary, any other women, or gentiles would have been left out of his story.

According to Matthew's Gospel, it was on a mountaintop in Galilee where the eleven met Jesus and continued to be afraid. He went ahead with his plan to commission them and send them forth to testify to what they had witnessed. "Go, therefore, and make disciples of all nations, baptizing them in the name of the Father, and of the Son, and of the Holy Spirit." He told them, "I am with you always, until the end of the age," the last words of Matthew's Gospel.

John wrote that these were only a part of the things Jesus did, and that he wrote them down so all might believe. It is at the end of this gospel when Jesus has a private discussion with Peter and puts him in charge. John closes by saying he is that disciple who testifies to all that he has written, and his testimony is true.

Following the appearance and commissioning, Mark and Luke both report that Jesus ascended into heaven from the Mount of Olives.

The story of the early days of Christianity continued in Acts of the Apostles. Only the chosen eleven were present for the Lord's ascension into heaven, but several others received the gift of the Holy Spirit on Pentecost. The apostolic brotherhood was formed and the disciples began to teach. Eventually they went their separate directions to carry the good news of Jesus Christ to all people.

In one well-known exchange between himself and Peter, Jesus asked his disciple three times if he loved him. Each time Peter, more insistently than before, proclaimed his love of the Lord, to which Jesus responded, "Feed my lambs," then, "Tend my sheep," and finally, "Feed my sheep." The Savior had again offered Peter three chances to deny him, but this time the apostle was strong in his conviction. "You know everything," he told the Lord, "so you know that I love you." Jesus told him about aging and that in old age he would not be able to go out to say and do the things he was able to do then, but mostly he was hinting at Peter's own death and its similarity to his, and gave one simple command: "Follow me."

John was nearby, and it was after his conversation with the Lord that Peter asked, "What about him?" John was the youngest among the apostles, and there was a genuine concern for his well-being. No one knew that Jesus, as he hung on the cross, had already committed John to adulthood when he asked the apostle to care for his mother. Legend holds that John may have been the only apostle not assassinated in some brutal way. His long life made it possible for him to see many things and to write them down.

Because of the age difference, John represented the thinking of another generation than the other apostles, and he saw a story unfold that was unique in its spiritual and metaphysical thinking. It was, for John, the truth of Jesus' message. He ended by telling his audience that if all the things Jesus said and did were written in detail, the whole world would not contain the books. For the faithful, Easter becomes more than one day of life. The second Sunday of Easter melds into the third, and then the fourth, and so on until every day is an expression of new life in the death and resurrection of Jesus the Lord.

Q *The gospels are testimony of things Jesus said and did. The stories vary slightly because they are written by four different witnesses for four different audiences. Their testimony is the good news of Jesus Christ. Do you read the gospels? Do you talk about the gospels with other people? Do you promote and encourage the study of the gospels?*

Love One Another

As the Easter season blossoms, there is new life in God's Church. Modern Christians have rites to proclaim the new life of spring. Parishes throughout the world have been celebrating the sacrament of baptism since the Easter Vigil, religious education teams are gearing up for first Communion and confirmation, and the annual wedding season is well under way. This is a presence of Christ which the contemporary Church is able to express openly. In the first century of the Christian era, celebrations were most often held in secret.

From their very first worship service when the apostles were hidden away in the upper room, they clung to the precepts Jesus had given…some, over and over again. Just as the pioneers of the Church faced supreme challenges, so does the Church today. The priest abuse scandal drove a wedge between the Church and her followers. When the cleansing and reconciliation is done, the clergy and the Church will be in greater shape. People may not want God or his Church in their lives, but the truth is, the sins Jesus predicted within the Church also go on outside of it.

Jesus made it all too clear how he felt about any infringement on the lives of others. He didn't define who or when; he meant everyone, all the time. The Lord repeated the essence of his command to the apostles right before and right after his death and resurrection. He wanted them to remember, "Love one another as I have loved you," and it applied to us all.

In the Old Testament Hebrew books, God revealed a plan for balancing life and faith. He told his people that the plan was for peace and harmony, that the suffering of humankind was brought on by humans themselves. God said he held a future full of hope for them. His instructions handed down to Moses centered on how humans love their God and each other. In the Book of Leviticus specifically, God gave instructions on how to love and care for the earth he provided. Again and again, through every prophecy and every action, the Father unveiled the layers of his love for people, until he gave the ultimate loving sacrifice in Jesus.

Jesus made it simple. There were really but two commandments: Love God with all you are and show that love by caring for one another. The greatest commandment or golden rule was not new. It is repeated throughout the Old Testament; Jesus just made it more clear. He was the ambassador of God's kingdom, and his purpose was to bring an understanding of what deep love, *agapé*, the unconditional love of God, was all about. He gave us a Church where we may meet with persons intent on care for and support of each other in the performance of God's will.

Knowing from past experience how difficult it was for people to carry out that plan, Jesus promised there will always be a power from God to help find the way, a Holy Spirit, a new attitude with peace and hope. He told the apostles and everyone who would ever hear his words that he would not leave people as orphans, that his presence would be with us until the end of the era. Jesus gave unconditional love and told his followers to spread that word, which is good news. Something we should want to do is built into us, and the good news of Jesus Christ is the answer to all things.

Every day is another Easter. It is a day of new hope. No matter what challenges confront us, loving without condition is mindfulness, an expression of how everything is a part of everything else. In the Gospel of Mary Magdalene, she wrote, the Teacher said, "All that is born and created, all elements of nature are interwoven and united together." To truly understand that concept and the human role within it is the understanding and peace God has always promised. It all comes down to "Love one another as I have loved you...."

Q *Agapé is love, not like humans love, but the way God loves. A Holy Spirit will show the way. It was words like these that Jesus left with his disciples. Part of the new life was to love all things more equally. Make an effort to feel more connected in love to the world around you. What does it mean to you to love unconditionally?*

Ascending

There is a clue to the wisdom Jesus handed over to his closest followers in the Acts of the Apostles, written by the same author as the Gospel of Luke. The evangelist informs readers that Jesus showed himself alive by "many proofs" throughout forty days following his suffering and death. Luke further says that Jesus talked about the kingdom of God. The author's first book contained what Jesus did and taught during his earthly ministry, right up to the ascension, which he reveals was done after Jesus gave instructions through the Holy Spirit to the chosen apostles. Jesus also told them to wait in Jerusalem until they personally received the Holy Spirit from the Father as he promised, after which the power of the Spirit would be with them as they carried the good news to the ends of the earth as his witnesses. Jesus specifically named Judea and Samaria as places they should go. These were not two names dropped at random. Judea was Canaan, the legendary Jewish Promised Land. Samaria was once part of that dream, but in Jesus' time, it was home to "the different people," the Samaritans. Jesus was telling them to take the gospel everywhere whether it be the land of friend or foe.

No one knew why the Lord took them to that place so early in the morning. They were on the east side of the Mount of Olives near Bethphage and facing in the direction of Bethany in the distance. It was still spring, but the conditions were windy and cold. At last the light of the morning sun appeared on the horizon, while Jesus was still talking, and as he told them to go out from Jerusalem to all places, he lifted up above the sunrise and was taken away on a cloud. The awestruck audience of apostles were not moved from their gawking after him until told to do so by two angels. The angels told the apostles that Jesus had been taken into heaven on a cloud, and when he returned it would be in the same manner.

The entourage then returned to Jerusalem.

In the upper room, the disciples of Jesus were gathered. There were the eleven apostles, Mary, his Mother, his brothers, Mary Magdalene and many others, all told one hundred and twenty followers. They petitioned the Lord together, read Scripture, and discussed it. Then, as they kept Jesus in their collective memory, they broke bread together.

Peter suddenly became the rock Jesus wanted him to be. He took charge and proclaimed to the others that the betrayal by Judas was known in the prophecy of David, and further, by that same tradition, there should be twelve apostles. He organized an election of a new apostle. There were some men who had been called by the Lord in the beginning of his ministry, and from them came Joseph Barsabbas and Matthias, two men equal to the eleven. After prayer and discernment, the lot was drawn by Matthias and he took the twelfth seat at their table.

The ascension is not celebrated in many American dioceses on the traditional Thursday that falls forty days after Easter, but rather the following Sunday. The faithful are still afforded the opportunity to recall Christ's message and put it to work in their own lives. In the dark of a late Saturday night, forty days ago, the Church ceremoniously recalled her history and Christ's triumph. After greeting the assembly gathered around a fire, the priest prepared the paschal candle and blessed it. His words reminded that Jesus was yesterday and today, beginning and end, Alpha and Omega. Christ is for every age. Since some of those same words appear scripturally in the Book of Revelation, the last volume of the Holy Bible, and similar thoughts regarding the Holy Trinity appear in the first chapter of Genesis, it is clearly understood that the presence of God in human lives took place long before we existed on earth and will continue long after.

Jesus' wish for his followers (as was the wish of the Father) was for peace and happiness. He called those who stand out in front to put themselves at the end of the line and to encourage those who are trapped at the back, unable to move beyond the trials of life, that they be lifted by a kindness of spirit and carried to the front. The instruction was not complicated; it was simply to care for one another without consideration for some sort of compensation.

The Lord was lifted up, and his disciples were left to finish what he had begun. Today's faithful are the heirs of that plan. The apostles created a creed and a set of principles, later written down and known as the Didache. Their mission, as it still is today, was to keep the justice and compassion of Christ alive. Through his death and resurrection and by his ascension to the Father, Jesus symbolized his move from last in death to first in the kingdom of God.

Q *By following Jesus' example, words, and deeds, the service to others and the sacrifice, the faithful are brought to journey through Christian life, and with humility and care are guided from last to first, ascending from the heart to the kingdom of God. Contemplate how you express love for God's whole creation. Does the Holy Spirit help you understand that God is love?*

Come, O Holy Spirit

As Jesus had promised, the Father would send to those who believed a share in his Holy Spirit the power to move a universe. This was every tool they'd need to carry out the work Christ left them to do.

As part of the "me" generation, many of today's churchgoers have stepped away from church being about God. Although it is about the faithful and their relationship to him, some people have just dropped God from the equation altogether and believe church is only about them. This seems to be a problem within most religions.

Saying one is "spiritual but not religious" is like saying the seeker wants the benefits but not the work to get them. A religion should help direct the spirit inside to the presence of God; true believers are both spiritual and religious. Spirituality is something to attain, and religion is a path to get there, but it requires action to ever be complete. Saint Paul wrote to the church in Colossae and told them, as God's beloved people, they were to have heartfelt compassion, kindness, humility, gentleness, and patience. He said they must bear with one another and forgive one another; as the Lord had forgiven them, so they also must do. Bind this all with love, the apostle instructed. Love is the bond of perfection, but they must let the peace of Christ control their hearts in one spirit and one body, and be thankful to God. He guided them to let the word of Christ live richly in the wisdom they shared with each other. Paul directed them to sing psalms and praise and to do all things in the name of the Lord Jesus, giving thanks to the Father through him.

The New Testament First Letter of John is an open homily to the entire Christian following. It was written by someone within the community of the apostle/evangelist, almost certainly a presbyter, very likely John's successor, and definitely a spokesman for the shaky, new Christian faith. The letter defines the difference between the spirit of God and any spirit that is not of God.

Faith is just that…faith.

John again calls the faithful to unity in a loving relationship with God through Jesus Christ. The document states that God is love. Whoever remains in love also remains in God and he in them. In this, the universal Church is told, love is brought to perfection. There is no doubt of God's love for his people. Some ask how a loving God allows us to suffer, but in truth, God allows us to be.

The spirit of love was something the disciples did not fully comprehend at the time of Jesus' ascension. They heard his words, but the meaning had not come to life in them as yet. This is similar to the experience of many churchgoers today who go through the motions without understanding the beauty of why.

How would his followers find all of this love and understanding? Jesus knew the road would not be easy. He assured them there was another face to God, an advocate, a Holy Spirit. The first community was hiding, just as they had been on the day he was resurrected and the week following. Their fear still hindered them because they didn't know, nor would they have understood, the words in John's yet-to-be-written first letter: Love knows no fear. Jesus would send a Holy Spirit to prove it and to make it possible for Christians to continue his loving ministry on earth.

Church attendance begins to fall off a little each week following Easter. As today's disciples, Christians are called to recognize the aftereffects of Christ's great sacrifice and every person's role in his ongoing mission. For the apostles and the other followers in Jesus' day, the hours were filled with community, prayer, and discernment. They tried to do the things he had taught them, but thus far, nothing turned out quite the way any of them expected.

The community was back in hiding. Some of today's community is back in hiding, and some of them won't return to church again until Christmas. Some of the original disciples gave their lives for the opportunity to worship in public. Today, worshipers in some parts of the world still face a very real danger. The persecution and rounding up of the followers of the new way was already taking place. Stephen, a disciple and representative to the Greeks, is called the first martyr of the church, but his assassination didn't happen until well after Pentecost. There is no evidence of any disciples executed before him, but within the community, fear and misunderstanding were all too real. Many feared for their lives.

Even though they were hiding, the apostles maintained their faith in Jesus and the God who sent him. They were afraid to begin their work among the people. The strength of the Holy Spirit wasn't theirs yet.

The disciples' prayer was complete, even if their understanding and spirit were not. They prayed what they believed and made ready to carry on Jesus' mission in the world. Most of all, God began to hone them to a sharpness that would allow the disciples to understand God's wisdom and share it in the world. They were a community with the ability to discuss and reason among themselves, to learn from one another.

It was a time of the greatest fear they had known and also the most promising, optimistic future with Christ. His disciples huddled together in the safety of each other and God's protection. Today in a time of fear and uncertainty, followers of Jesus should be huddled together in prayer and worship of the Lord.

Q *The Holy Spirit animates the will and creation of God. Even in the worship the disciples shared, an action was commencing, and a spirit developing among them. Consider your role as a participant at Mass. Do you pray out loud and in silence? Do you sing the hymns of faith? Do you listen to the word of God? Do you feel Christ's love in the breaking of the bread? Do you feel the spirit?*

And They Were Filled With the Holy Spirit

Every age, every decade has had its defining moment, some in chaos, but relatively few in peace. More wars, military police actions, revolutions, and coups have taken place on the earth since World War II than are recorded in all of history before that time. Many people don't trust each other as they once did. In 2010, the Gulf of Mexico was covered in oil, but people might not have noticed it much in places like Haiti or China, or anyplace where the poor are still digging out of a natural disaster. The insatiable thirst for power and energy devastated Japan the following year, when unsafe nuclear facilities were rocked by earthquakes and spilled radioactivity into land and sea. The plan for future oil exploration includes earthquakes triggered by humans deep underground. The world can be a frightening place.

It was a different era with some of the same problems but many that weren't. Judea was one of many lands dominated by the Roman Empire. It was a troubling time leading up to the first Pentecost fifty days after Jesus' resurrection. Already there were factions forming in the community with differing opinions, testing each other's faith about what the Lord did, including how (if) he died and was resurrected. Drawing together such diversity was a challenge from the word go.

What if the arrival of the Holy Spirit never took place? How long would the apostles have waited before they themselves ventured away from the hideout, and maybe even from Jerusalem? Jesus didn't give them a timeline, and many of them came from Galilee. It was different following Jesus when he wasn't around anymore. The apostles had their doubts, and certainly they shared them among themselves. They held together, the same disciples who gathered following the ascension, and in their presence, the defining moment of the Church arrived.

The apostles were asking each other, "What do we do?" At the same moment, the wind outside intensified, roared noisily from the sky, and blew open the shudders of the upper room. Was this the same wind that passed over the formless wasteland that would become the earth in the Father's hands, as stated in the first verses of Genesis? This spirit was the part of God that turned thought into action. Tongues of fire peeled away like petals from a flaming rose and descended, coming to rest over the heads of those who were gathered. They were immediately filled with the Holy Spirit of understanding, as if Jesus' words had been collected, awaiting a special key to be opened like a treasure chest. The disciples began to speak knowledgeably in different languages so they could take the meaning of the gospel to the ends of the earth.

A crowd gathered outside because of the cacophonic sound of the wind. The disciples emerged from the upper room and began preaching in unison. Everyone assembled was mentally directed to hear the sound of his/her own language. They were bewildered by what they were witnessing. Some among them sought prophecy or some faith-filled explanation, and others thought the disciples were drunk or play-acting.

What happened that day was not a new holy spirit, but a renewed wisdom, courage, and perseverance to live Christ-like. There was a new covenant, a new attitude, and a Holy Spirit to be the guide for those apostles and all the faithful yet to come. Fear had washed away, and the witnesses of the Lord stepped out of the shadows with vigor and promise. That call is for all today, as well. God's plan is not new but is to be renewed. The people of faith can renew and rebuild by acting in truth and spirit. The disciples did it; and Peter took the reins.

Pentecost is the celebration of the birth of that Church. Without a communal Holy Spirit, the disciples would never have been able to withstand the worldly forces that could have toppled their Church and their lives. How little things have changed.

Church is described as the whole body of Christian believers. In that context, Church is representative of all Christian denominations. Despite the differences that separate one Christian faith from another, there is a unity in Jesus Christ. If an abuse takes place it is hurtful to all. Every personality helps to make up Church and is responsible for carrying their share to see that it is made better, not torn apart. The same Holy Spirit that came to the apostles was given to all who believe in God's ways and their expression through Jesus Christ.

Q *Sometimes we are slow to take action even knowing it is the right course. The disciples had absorbed Jesus' words and deeds, but they were slow to spread the fire of his love. Do you have times when you are slow to respond when you know what needs to be done? Do you pray to the Holy Spirit of God for guidance and then listen for his instructions?*

Peter

If anyone had cornered Simon Peter following the miracle of Pentecost and tried to coerce him into admitting he was friends with the man called Jesus, he would have certainly responded differently than he did on Good Friday. For Peter and the other disciples a great miracle had taken place following the blessing, when the Holy Spirit descended upon them in the early morning, and their rapture lasted well after dark. In the modern Church, the Easter season is over at sunset on Pentecost Sunday.

Peter was outside with the other apostles when they began to preach in foreign tongues that morning, and he heard the jeering and the teasing of those who did not understand. He bellowed out to them that these apostles were not drunk or foolish, after all, it was only nine o'clock in the morning. There were those in the crowd who didn't understand but wanted to know more, and they welcomed the big man's words.

Peter began an oration unlike anything he had done before. He was instantly transformed, and the leader of the new way recapitulated the prophets and psalms, and thus began what is known as "kerygma," the Proclamation. He chastised the Jews, who were listening, for their part, not only in encouraging the death of the Lord, who they knew had been sent by God because of the things he did, but also that they turned him over to Romans, enemies of the Jews, to carry out the treacherous deed. It was a friendly reminder, with just the right dosage of fire and brimstone to put the "fear of God" into the crowd. It was a speech like nothing they'd heard since Jesus addressed them. Peter was speaking with a new knowledge of truth and understanding; he was telling it the way the Lord would have done. The end result, according to Acts of the Apostles, is that three thousand converts were baptized that single day. The Scripture continues to tell even more converts came to the apostles virtually on a daily basis thereafter.

The work and the union of the Holy Trinity was completed when the Holy Spirit descended over the witnesses of Christ, baptized them with fire, and sent them forth with understanding as promised by Jesus and gifted by the Father, the complete equation of God's divine plan. To achieve our human connection with this mystery of faith, intuitive knowledge is needed more than a physical understanding.

All of the major prayers of the Eucharistic Liturgy refer to the persons and the works of each member of the Holy Trinity: the Gloria, the Nicene Creed, and the Eucharistic Prayer, which ends with a doxology, an acknowledgment of the united effort of the Father, whose plan of creation included peaceful life for humanity, secured by the Son, who made his great sacrifice come to life for humanity through the Eucharist, and the Holy Spirit, whose guidance leads to a faithful heart for humanity. This is the culmination of what was always God's intention.

Peter stressed to the crowd that despite their actions, Jesus was raised from the dead by the will of God, and the apostle sang to them from Psalm 16, a prophetic affirmation that this was true. "I keep the Lord always before me...my heart is glad, my soul rejoices, and my body dwells securely...I will not be abandoned...you, Lord, show me the path of life."

He went on to say that David, who had written the psalms, even though he was mortal man who died and was buried near where they stood, had made a covenant with God, and the Lord told him that a descendant of his would be the resurrected Messiah. Peter reminded the apostles among them that they were all witnesses to that resurrection. Then he recalled how Jesus promised a holy spirit from the Father, and on that day poured out that promise to them. He bellowed out to the crowd how God had raised to Lord and Messiah this Jesus whom they crucified.

The community that had developed while the disciples were in hiding and then were given to understanding by the Holy Spirit was not to be separated in spirit again. In the beginning they all stayed together to learn from the apostles, to worship and pray, and to break the bread of thanksgiving. They were awestruck by the wonders and signs from God, worked through the apostles, and they began to heal minds and bodies.

Peter and the others knew things they'd never known before; they were wise and able to carry the mission of the believers, which had only just begun. Psalm 8 reminded them, "You have made him little less than a god, crowned him with glory and honor. You have given him rule over the works of your hands, put all things at his feet."

The disciples of the Lord were given a strength and power that comes only from God. Those same gifts await those who are ready to receive them with a contrite heart. Those who came forward to repent and be baptized were many. They were what the disciples did the rest of the Church's first day.

As he had taken charge in word, so too did Peter take the lead in action. As his ministry began, with John at his side, Peter went among the people of Jerusalem. The community of disciples had begun to work their way back into the city, and they joined in worship at the Temple.

Q *Think of the Holy Trinity, the three faces of God. The Father is the King, the Overseer, the Creator. Jesus is the Teacher, the Example, the Sacrifice. The Holy Spirit is the Doer, the Expression of God that brings thought to action. Do you feel an interaction with the Holy Trinity in your life?*

The Apostles Among the People

As Peter and John arrived near the Temple, they encountered a beggar at the Beautiful Gate. He had been crippled from birth, and it was his place to beg outside the "rich" entrance to the Temple whenever there was a worship service. People passed by the man, some tossing coins into his satchel, and as Peter and John approached the gate, he called out to them, asking for their contribution. The apostles stopped and looked intently at the beggar as Peter called him to "look at us." It was customary for the beggar to look down and not into the faces of the wealthy patrons, but he raised his head at Peter's request, to see what gift he was to receive.

Peter told the beggar, "I have neither silver nor gold, but what I have, I give you freely in the name of Jesus Christ, the Nazorean." Then he told the man to rise and walk. The apostle took his right hand and began to help him up, but the beggar's legs immediately grew strong, and he finished leaping to his feet on his own. He walked about joyously and even went into the Temple with the two apostles. He created a commotion inside, still dancing in reaction to his blessing from God. Some of those who had seen him before watched in amazement at his jubilation.

The formerly crippled beggar could get along on his own, but he continued to cling to Peter in a part of the Temple known as Solomon's Portico. That columned porch provided a large viewing area, and many gathered to get a look at this miraculous being. Peter saw their numbers and began to speak to all of them. He told the Israelites that they should not be so amazed and certainly not think that he and John had done this of their own power. Peter said the God of Abraham, Isaac, Jacob, and all their ancestors had glorified Jesus whom the Jews testified against, even when Pilate was prepared to release him. This same man, "the author of life" who they had put to death was raised up by the Father, and it was through Jesus that this beggar, a man of faith, was given health.

Once he finished berating them, Peter became more consoling. He told them he was aware they had acted out of ignorance, just as their leaders had, in condemning the Lord though they had seen his works and had heard the words of the prophets. He called all of them to conversion that they might be renewed by God. He quoted from the early books attributed to Moses and showed that even then, Jesus was prophesied.

As Peter continued to talk about the resurrection of the Messiah, Sadducees rounded up the priests and the Temple guards and came forward to confront the apostles. The result was Peter and John being taken for an overnight stay in prison. As they were taken away, the number of believers in the crowd began to swell, and the three thousand they had converted on the first day became five thousand with this incident.

Annas, the high priest, had taken control of the proceedings of the Sanhedrin after the fiasco involving Jesus, whose body still wasn't accounted for. With Caiaphas and the other members at his side, he had but one question for Peter and John when they were brought before the council: "By what authority or name have you done this?"

Peter was strong and blessed with the Holy Spirit. He spoke up and told them, if they were trying to discover how the apostles had done this good deed for a cripple, then they should let all the people of Israel know that it was through the name of Jesus Christ, the Nazorean, who they had crucified but who was raised up by God. Peter continued to preach to the priests, and they were astonished by his words, previously thinking he was uneducated and ordinary. Then the crippled man walked forward and stood with the two apostles. The priests had seen the miracle themselves and had to make a decision. After consultation, the priests told the apostles that they could go free on the condition they would not speak in the name of Jesus again. Peter and John didn't budge. Peter gave the council no promise other than: The apostles would tell everyone what they'd seen and heard.

The Sanhedrin was outraged by the boldness of the apostles. They went into council again. When they returned the priests issued a reprimand, told Peter and John not to do anything in the name of Jesus, and then let them go free. The two apostles returned to the other disciples and told what had happened. From that day forward the community was strong in the Holy Spirit, and like-minded disciples continued to live together in worship and prayer, in breaking the bread, and caring for each others' needs.

Q *Just as in the days of the first disciples, the faithful today are called to the ongoing care of each other. Churches and organizations lead in helping the needy, but what about Jesus' personal call to relieve the hungry and the thirsty, shelter the homeless, clothe the naked, welcome the stranger, and to care for the needs of the imprisoned and infirmed? Think about and then make a commitment to do one of those things in some way.*

James

James, John, Mary (Miriam), and even Jesus (Yeshua) were all very common names in Jesus' time, and because there are some of each who actively participate in the telling of the New Testament, there is often confusion as to who's who. Precious little of the disciple James' life has been authenticated. He is the James who, for centuries, has been referred to by some as the brother of Jesus. The translation could also mean he was a cousin, so the standard connotation is "the relative of Jesus." Acts of the Apostles and the gospels specifically call some other men the brothers of Jesus, but they do not name them.

James was not even one of the twelve apostles, but he certainly was a disciple of some measure. He was the first bishop of the Church in Jerusalem as the disciples began spreading out to other places. There is a letter in the New Testament, sometimes called "the perfect law of freedom," attributed to him but more likely authored by a Greco-Roman-educated disciple of James. The Letter of James addresses how Christians are to carry out the call of God's love in their lives, how to live Christian.

The letter went out to the apostles and all disciples, and reached the churches throughout Asia Minor, Palestine, and Rome. The churches had become lax and some had strayed from Jesus' core teachings about twenty-five years after his death and resurrection.

James' instruction launched a renewal of the principles of their faith. The author instructed: Faith alone is not salvation unless it is supported by works.

James began by reminding everyone of the joy to be gained in human trials and tests of their faith. He said these things produce perseverance, and enough perseverance leads to spiritual perfection and completeness. James tells the churches how to prayerfully ask for something. God will give when there is faith without doubt. It is essential to approach the Lord with one mind and certainty. Indecision causes one to be tossed about like high wind tosses the sea.

The letter draws a line between the humble and the lofty. It recalls from Isaiah that grass withers and flowers fade, but God's word lasts forever. Worldly things also fade away, the letter says. It calls for people to persevere in the face of temptation, as well. Temptation does not come from God but from inner human desires, which materialize as sin. All good things come from the Father, and he has chosen humans to be first among the creatures. Anger and wrath do not serve God's purpose.

A strong emphasis in James' letter is on doing righteous things. He said, to hear the word and not act accordingly is like looking in a mirror and then forgetting what one looks like when he walks away from the reflection. Religion that is pure and undefiled before God is a call to care for others and to keep one's self unstained.

The writer said, one who looks into "the perfect law of freedom" and who perseveres does not hear and forget, but instead acts, and he will be blessed in what he does.

Make no distinction between people. If a man came into one's home in fine clothes next to another in shabby clothes, and he is given the royal treatment while the poor man is told to sit at the feet of the house Master, that homeowner would be guilty of making a distinction, setting himself up as a judge, symbolic of evil intentions. God chose the poor as recipients of his kingdom because of their faith, and to give them less than a rich man is to dishonor them.

It is the rich and worldly who oppress, not the poor. If one fulfills the supreme law in Scripture, "You shall love your neighbor as yourself," that person has done well, while the one who disobeys God's law has sinned. James says there is no greater or lesser commandment among the ten but reaffirms the greatest commandment, to love God with heart, soul, and mind, and to show that love by the way we care for each other.

James described how destructive the tongue could be to the community and even suggested that some of the disciples were not called to teach but should fulfill their mission in other ways. Using an image of a little flame that became a forest fire, he explained how the whole church can be judged because of the wrong thing being said, or because an angry word prevented them from persevering in the face of a human trial. The disciple stressed that blessing and cursing come from the same mouth, but as a stream doesn't pour forth two kinds of water from the same source, neither does a human have to speak in both manners.

Yet another part of James' instructions talks about true wisdom. He asked his audience, who among them was wise and understanding, and he told them to show their works by a humble, good life that comes from true wisdom. Covetousness and selfish ambition do not come from God but are an evil product of earthly desires. His lesson reminded that real wisdom comes from above, and it is first of all pure, then peaceful. That spirit is gentle, compliant, merciful, and in essence, James was speaking of the fruits yielded by the Holy Spirit. True wisdom is constant and sincere.

Q *James' letter came at a time when many in the fledgling Church were complacent. It is a most solid reminder that conversion to the way, the truth, and the life in Jesus is constant, a goal with which you don't reach a point and graduate. Do you try to be a better person in Christ each day? Do you try to know him more each day?*

The Hard Lessons

The Letter of Saint James addressed war, conflict, and division, asking rhetorically, "Where do wars come from?" He answered his own question: The source of these troubles is human passion and desire. Covetousness drives people away from God because they did not ask him for what they want, but rather designed to take it willfully by any other means. Acting on those worldly passions is like breaking a marriage bond with God, to be like "adulterers," in the writer's words. He who is overly attached to the worldly things makes "an enemy of God." The Lord desires for all to have happiness, but selfishness and human pride fight against it. The Lord resists the proud and gives grace to the humble.

"Draw near to God, and he will draw near to you," James informed. He told the Christian believers to be clean of hand and heart, to focus on what they want of God, and to be humble before him to receive his grace. He warned them not to speak evil of one another, for in so doing they speak evil of God's law.

James also made the people aware. He'd heard there were disciples among them who set up businesses in some towns and profited from them, rather than being about the mission of the Lord, to spread the good news. He reminded them, they may not have tomorrow to change their ways; God is here and now. Then in a phrasing known as the Condition of James, the disciple writes, one should say, "If the Lord wills it, we shall live to do this or that."

He challenged all followers of the Lord to know and do the right thing. For the rich, the landowners, and employers, who gather their riches on earth at the expense of those they employ and fail to do the right things with the wealth they gain, those things stand witness before God. It is clear throughout the Bible that the Lord is the champion of the oppressed, and he scorns those who are rich at the expense of the poor. James reaffirms that.

The author told the people to have patience until the Lord has come. The image he uses is that of a farmer who plants and nurtures, and waits and waits for the rains to come, until the "precious fruit of the earth" is ready for harvest. Be firm of heart, adds James, and be ready for the Lord to come. Don't complain about one another or be judged likewise. He called to example the hardship and patience of the prophets. For those who persevere see the purpose of the Lord who comes with compassion and mercy. Do not overburden with the abuse of oaths, but let "yes" mean "yes" and "no" mean "no," to avoid condemnation.

In the last few paragraphs of the letter, the writer turns to the prayer and ritual of the fledgling churches. He tells them that anointing of the sick should be a priority. If anyone is suffering, pray. If one is in good spirits, sing praise to God. But if anyone is sick, someone should call the priests to anoint the person with oil and pray over him in the name of the Lord. This rite will assist in preparing the person to be raised up by God, and his sins will be forgiven.

The overall view of confession is also considered. James tells the disciples to confess to one another and to pray for each other's healing. He explains that fervent prayer is very powerful, using Elijah as an example of earnest prayer; the prophet stopped torrential rain for three and a half years. When he prayed again for rain to resume, the skies brought forth the moisture, and there was a bountiful harvest.

Finally, James ends the letter rather abruptly by telling every disciple that one who brings back a sinner from his error and untruth, his sins will be forgiven, and he will be restored to life. This is a fundamental of caring for each other, and the last word of a Bible letter that really does spell out the action a Christian should follow.

> Q *Overall, the Letter of James states, "Faith is not a spectator sport." He told people for all times to be active in the things the Lord has shown them to do. Consider how you express your faith and how God's love works through you. Do you feel more enhanced to step forward and walk the way Jesus did? Do you believe you are a good example to others? Be an active faith participant. They'll know we are Christians by our love.*

Part III: Every Day With Jesus

The Remembrance

A sixty-something man was recounting the history of more than half a century ago, when he was not only a student at Holy Ghost Catholic School in Albuquerque, New Mexico, but also a very dedicated altar boy. Servers were all boys in the 1950s. One story he told was about the Corpus Christi procession that took place, probably in 1958. It rambled through the streets of the city and ended at the Cathedral of the Immaculate Conception downtown. One of the boy's duties was to transport a lit incense pot in his grandmother's car. The crowd in town was heavy and the traffic moved slowly. As the boy's grandma meandered through the crush, the incensor burned a hole in the carpet of the old Plymouth's back floor. His mother and grandmother managed to douse the smoldering, smelly rug while the boy made it to the procession on time.

With all of that going on, the man's most fond remembrance was the procession itself. He said it was like a magnificent parade. In those days, parades were big in Albuquerque. The former altar boy couldn't remember for sure what streets they traveled on, but he easily recalled the huge crowd that lined them. New Mexico wasn't more Catholic back then, but people of faith were surely more demonstrative.

In 1960, the boy moved from Albuquerque with his parents and didn't return for several years. When he went back as an adult, he became very active in the church and noticed that the big citywide procession was gone, with no idea how long it'd been that way. Listed as one of the Holy Days of Obligation in the *Catechism of the Catholic Church*, Corpus Christi, the Most Holy Body and Blood of Christ, is one of those special days that has been transported to Sunday annually, partially to assure attendance at the Eucharistic Liturgy on a special day of remembrance. It is fitting that the celebration is the third week following Pentecost and the Most Holy Trinity in a sequence that completes the framework of Church.

All was not lost for the man. He told his story to the pastor he served with. The priest was very liturgically aware, and for the next two years the parish had a procession through the vast church grounds in honor of the Body and Blood of Christ. Children brightened the pathway by scattering rose petals before the monstrance that bore the Blessed Sacrament. The community gathered at a stone altar in an outdoor grotto for appropriate prayer and Scripture. Some parishes, not only in New Mexico, but throughout the universal Church, continue to honor the tradition within their own communities, but as it is with many other old rituals, a few less congregations participate each year.

The former altar server said that as he got more involved in liturgy, he was able to take classes from and through the Archdiocese of Santa Fe. In one of those classes, there was a video presentation featuring Kathleen Hughes, RSCJ, educator, author, and lecturer. She was speaking of Jesus' words spoken during the consecration, specifically, "Do this in memory of me." Then she asked, what is the "this" we are asked to do. The man said she had raised for him a question that should be central to every Catholic.

Surely, the Lord was talking about something more than remembering the Eucharist. The bread and wine become a living symbol, the substances of Body and Blood. The sacrament commemorates its own creation at the Last Supper in the hands of Jesus, who continues with the Holy Spirit and the power of the Father to bring life to those who share and believe, even today. He called the faithful to take on his life in the bread and share in the covenant that was written in his blood. The "this," that God's people are called to is what they do after they have been filled with the presence of Christ.

Jesus had long since revealed to his followers that the greatest commandment was to love God with heart, soul, and mind, and to demonstrate that love by the way they cared for one another. This was only the groundwork for what he would share at the Last Supper and what would become the disciples' way of life after Pentecost. "Take and eat; this is my body," Jesus said. He was telling them to take in the power of his life and to fill their unnamed hunger with the Lord.

Q *Recall your history as a member of the Church. Surely there will be times that are more important and more vivid in your memory. Then recall a tradition you've either seen or heard about. Do you believe all these things—the tradition, culture, and custom of the Church—add to your ability to sense and to pray?*

The Bread of Life

The gospels read at the Solemnity of the Most Holy Body and Blood of Christ over the three-year cycle reflect different eucharistic moments. First is John's description of Jesus as the Living Bread from the Bread of Life discourse. In the second year, Mark's version of the institution of the Eucharist at the Last Supper is proclaimed. Thirdly, Luke reveals the story of how Christ fed the multitudes with fish, bread, and the good news of the kingdom of God. This event established the ability of Jesus to feed the masses with himself, through the will of the Father and the power of his Holy Spirit. He fed real hunger.

Chapter six of John's Gospel is known as the Bread of Life discourse. Read every three years, it is typical of John in that it has layers of teaching. The lesson is very much what the Church believes about the Eucharist and Jesus' presence within it. Eucharist means "give thanks." It is the glory and praise to God through the gift of his Son. This gospel chapter tells why.

Jesus had been talking with Jews who claimed to ascribe to the Law of Moses but followed it very loosely. They were angered that he cured someone on the Sabbath, and he asked why their praise of each other was worth more to them than seeking praise from God.

Jesus was looking to get away from the debate. He crossed the Sea of Galilee into unknown territory, the land of the gentiles. Many of the Jews had seen him cure the sick, including the man who had been ill for thirty-eight years, the one cured on the Sabbath, and they arrogantly followed Jesus to the other side of the sea. It was nearing the time of Passover, but not in the year when Jesus suffered, died, and was resurrected.

Jesus made his way to the top of the mountain with the apostles and they engaged in contemplative prayer as they prepared for their Passover journey. When the prayer had ended and the Lord raised his eyes, he saw throngs of people all over the hill and valley, waiting for him to speak. Jesus formulated a plan to feed the crowd and then asked Philip where they might buy that amount of food. Philip told him there wasn't enough money among them to do that, and the Lord turned to Andrew. The apostle confessed the only food he could find was a carried by a kid who had five barley loaves (the grain of the poor) and two fish. Jesus told Andrew to have the people recline on the grass of the vast hillside and meadow. There were about five thousand of them. Jesus took the meager offering, gave thanks and praise to the Father, and asked the disciples to distribute food to all those on the grass. When everyone was full and the leftovers gathered, they filled twelve baskets. Jew and gentile alike seemed to agree at that point: He was the prophet, the one from God who came into this world. Knowing that they intended to honor him and make him an earthly king, Jesus retreated alone back to the top of the mountain, where he returned to his unceasing prayer.

Jesus wanted to quell the fear in the crowd that they might not eat by showing them that God does indeed provide. He wanted them to be comfortable while he taught. Jesus was no stranger to using the dinner table as a place to preach the kingdom of God. Because he gathered Jew and gentile, rich and poor, young and old that day, it was a demonstration of the universality of the Lord. He certainly proved that there was always enough of him to go around. This was indeed a preview to the Eucharist at the Last Supper. Jesus fed the simple needs of the people, and then he fed their spirit.

John writes that Jesus stayed on the mountain until after dark. As those who had gathered began to return home, or fell asleep in the meadow under the stars, their bellies and their minds still absorbing what they had been a part of, the apostles commissioned a boat and began to sail away.

They had lost Jesus!

No one knew where he was, and because of a storm rising on an already treacherous Sea of Galilee, they couldn't wait to start out for Capernaum. Jesus had more to teach them, but first they had to make a voyage of faith. When they were out on the sea, as the weather got worse and worse, they were afraid for their lives. Jesus appeared to them moving across the surface of the sea, and they became even more afraid, thinking he was a ghost. Jesus told them it was he, and they were about to help him into the boat when the weather cleared, and they were already at their destination. Faith in the Lord can steer one through any storm.

Whatever the test for the apostles, they apparently fared well enough that Jesus deemed them ready for his revelation as the Bread of Life. The gospels speak with different meaning for different people; some hear only a special part. The feeding of the multitudes is the only miracle that is written about in all four gospels. It is the key to the message Jesus was leading up to...God loves abundantly through Jesus Christ, the Bread by which we gain true life. Faith in him will care for us and sustain us always.

Ever since Jesus, Christians have celebrated the remembrance of the first Eucharist as the centerpiece of worship. The assembled faithful celebrate the four parts of the Emmaus journey. They tell their story, what is known as the Penitential Rite, exposing their faults and humanness to one another, the communion of saints, and to God himself. They ask for forgiveness from one another and pray that the Lord, the Christ, will have mercy. Then, as Jesus did for the two disciples on the road, spokespersons reveal the Word of God and how it pertains to human life here and now. Through the Penitential Rite and the Liturgy of the Word the faithful have been drawn into one body. As the two disciples felt the closeness, they broke bread with Jesus, who they didn't recognize. They were extending true Christian life, service, and hospitality to another human without regard for who or what he was. Jesus consecrated the symbolic bread and wine into his actual living Body and Blood. Then and now, those who receive him in their hearts are suddenly able to recognize him and know his living presence within.

Receiving him in the bread and wine and becoming one body in Christ with one another was not the finish. It was the quickening for the ministry ahead. Like the two disciples who ran back to Jerusalem, proclaiming the triumph of God, the faithful even today are called to continue the proclamation, to live and to share the "good news" of Jesus Christ, and to be strengthened for that mission by the Holy Eucharist, the Bread of Life.

It may only be a small piece of dry, unleavened bread—and barely enough wine to wet the lips—but as the Body and Blood of Jesus, it is a monumental remembrance of God's constant love, the unity he has with his people through his Son, with the power and wisdom of the Holy Spirit, and no less a call to action by service and prayer. Every day is the remembrance of the love and life within the most holy Body and Blood of Christ. We walk with Jesus in the end that we may also walk with him in the beginning. We are drawn into sharing the last days of his human life so that we may also be there for the first days of new life in the Lord. Go forth and share his love.

If you liked *Carry on in Faith*, you may also like these titles from Liguori Publications...

Seven Words of Jesus and Mary

Lessons on Cana and Calvary

Fulton Sheen

ISBN: 978-0-7648-0708-4

Analyzes the relation between the seven recorded words that Mary spoke in the gospels and the seven last words of her Son as he hung on the cross. Offers solace for the fears and dilemmas of today's Christian by interpreting the gospel from the intertwined perspective of Mother and Son.

How Can I Find God?

The Famous and the Not-So-Famous Consider the Quintessential Question

James Martin

ISBN: 978-0-7648-0090-0

This vibrant collection brings together an array of voices addressing the question of how one might approach the search for God. With contributors from many faith traditions, this book will be of value to all who seek to answer the question, "How Can I Find God?"

Handbook for Today's Catholic

Revised Edition

ISBN: 978-0-7648-1220-0

Presented in easy-to-understand language, with content divided into Beliefs, Practices, Prayers, and Living the Faith, and fully indexed to the *Catechism of the Catholic Church*. Perfect for RCIA and parish adult faith-formation groups, high school religious-education classes, inquirers into the Catholic faith, and people who want to have the essentials of Catholicism at their fingertips.

To Order Visit Your Local Bookstore
Call 800-325-9521 • Visit liguori.org

Liguori Publications offers many titles as eBooks through leading distributors such as Amazon, Barnes & Noble, Kobo, and iTunes.